th Woodville   Margaret Hughes   Æthelflæd

Fanny Mendelssohn

...Smythe   Sa...   ...svig...

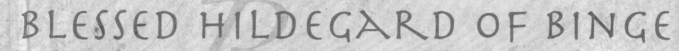

...Borneo...

BLESSED HILDEGARD OF BINGE

...nt Burney

...gifu   SACAGAWEA Thaïs

Bessie Coleman   Queen Sammurama...

Courtesans   Nora Hildebrandt

...nia Lewis   Maid Lilliard

...Post Cecily Mary Hamilt...

Fannie Farmer   Emma de Bu...

...y Wortley Montagu   MIMI GARNEAU

Vishpala

...t Girl   Tattooed Ladies

Marie Antoinette

Anne Bracegirdle   Queen Zenobia

...Ælfgifu

...ightinga...

Heroines & Harridans

Heroines & Harridans

Sandi Toksvig &
Sandy Nightingale

(Who have been working on this project for some time)

The Robson Press

First published in Great Britain in 2012
by The Robson Press (an imprint of Biteback Publishing Ltd.)

A book from The Two Sandies:
Sandi Toksvig writes the words.
Sandy Nightingale paints the pictures.

ISBN 978 1849 54 3385

Design, art direction, token male & tea-maker:
Gary Day-Ellison (www.day-ellison.com)

Printed and bound in Great Britain by Butler, Tanner & Dennis

'*Lydia, the Tattooed Lady*' Words and Music by Harold Arlen and E. Y. Harburg © 1939.
Reproduced by permission of EMI Music Publishing Ltd, London W8 5SW

Westminster Tower
3 Albert Embankment
London SE1 7SP

www.therobsonpress.com

This book is dedicated to our games mistresses
who wasted their time.

DANE
SANDI
TOKSVIG

Preface

It is not by chance that the relation of matters in the past is called 'History'. It is, generally, 'his story', with many men doing grand things while the women stayed home to make the soup. *Heroines & Harridans* attempts in a small way to redress the balance. Here is an eccentric and entirely personal mélange of the many women who were terrifically good fun, may have shaped the world but then disappeared into obscurity.

It is a tale of exemplary eccentricity (generally British), some very bad behaviour (occasionally American) and rather peculiar love lives (some corking aristocrats).

There are no soup recipes in this book.

Contents

A Capricious Collection

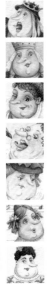

"*Variety is the soul of pleasure.*"
Aphra Behn

CHOICE IS A MARVELLOUS THING. How splendid to sit of a sunny afternoon before a three-tiered cake stand rich with offerings and take a moment to consider which delicate delight takes one's fancy. So it has been with this book. The array of glorious women at our disposal whose lives we might have chewed over has been overwhelming.

In the end it was too big a selection of cakes and we had to choose. Sometimes we chose carefully, occasionally we were capricious but all the while we knew that we were merely gliding over the surface of a stand laden with possibilities. Some of our females are famous, like Elizabeth I, while others are shamefully overlooked women who deserve to be re-discovered and enjoyed. We have tried to put the spotlight on those who have sometimes soared out of the pages of history. No one who ever sits down at a computer should forget Augusta Lovelace and every woman should sing the praises of the composer Dame Ethel Smyth, who conducted an orchestra of suffragettes with a toothbrush from her prison cell window. In addition there is a fine selection of women called Fanny and a cluster of women whose name begin Æ. In a bid for controversy we have also included the odd woman whose life some have tried to deny entirely such as Pope Joan, the only Pope to give birth during an official ceremony.

The book is stuffed with splendid art and a few facts but not enough to give you a headache. It is the *Hello* version of the past but hopefully with more jokes. There is also one woman with her top off in the middle of the book. This is intended to attract the reader more given to car-tyre calendars than history.

We love our selection of women but it does seem a shame to have overlooked, for example, the painters Mary Moser and Angelika Kauffman for they have been overlooked before. Both Mary and Angelika were celebrated artists of the eighteenth century. They were also the two female founder members of the Royal Academy of Art, which began in 1768. When, however, a great portrait of all the original members was done it was only the founding fathers who took pride of place. Mary and Angelika appear as bas-reliefs on the wall behind the men.

How awful to have passed by Murasaki Shikibu, who in eleventh-century Japan wrote the world's first novel. It should surprise no one that 'Murasaki Shikibu' is a nickname. We don't know her real name. How about the Grimké sisters, Angelina and Sarah, who spoke out against slavery and for women's rights back in the 1830s before anyone else had thought of it? Surely we were tempted by the great German-British astronomer Caroline Herschel who in the eighteenth century became the first woman to receive a salary for services to science? Who could forget Phyllis Wheatley, who was born in 1753 in Senegal and went on to become America's first African-American poet? Or Harriet Tubman, who from 1850 until the American Civil War helped over 300 fugitive slaves escape? Or the Venetian, Elena Cornaro, who in 1678 became the first woman in the world to graduate with a degree? Or Lil Hardin Armstrong, the bandleader from the 1930s who declared "*I was just born to swing, that's all.*"? Or Aphra Benn who in 1670 became the first professional female writer or . . .

At least we can bask in Aphra Benn's words when she said "*Variety is the soul of pleasure.*" Virginia Woolf wrote of her that, "*All women together, ought to let flowers fall upon the grave of Aphra Behn . . . for it was she who earned them the right to speak their minds.*" So, thank you Aphra and thank you to all heroines and harridans everywhere.

A personal thanks –

We are endlessly grateful to the genius Gary Day-Ellison who kept asking for new words and artwork and polished the book design to perfection. This is a book about women but we must not forget that we can also work well with the boys. Co-operation is the key. It was a fellow called Allen Gant who in 1953, at the request of his wife, invented tights. Women have rejoiced in the death of the garter belt and should praise Mr Gant. Let's not forget, however, that it was his wife Ethel who sewed the first pair from some pants and stockings and that it was the American actress Julie Newmar who improved the product by getting a patent for a 'shaping' pantyhose which made "your derriere look like an apple instead of a ham sandwich". There is not a woman in the world who doesn't suspect that it was a man who invented the notion that 'one size' fits all.

Sandi Toksvig

Sandy Nightingale

Alice B. Toklas

1877—1967

THE IRONY FOR ARTISTS AND writers who wish to be avant-garde or ahead of the game (a mode of life recommended for any creative wishing to be remembered) is that the ideal time to do so is behind us. Early-twentieth-century Paris was terribly avant-garde with artists turning urinals into important works of art (Marcel Duchamp), painters deciding everything looked better in cubes (Georges Braque and Pablo Picasso) and writers who liked nothing better than popping into a bit of a literary salon (Ernest Hemingway, Thornton Wilder). At the heart of all this desperately forward thinking was an American woman called Gertrude Stein and at Gertrude's own heart stood Alice B. Toklas.

Alice was born in San Francisco, California in 1877. She grew up to study music and in 1907 went to Paris. On her very first day she met Gertrude Stein. Gertrude was also American and brilliant. So brilliant that she spent all her time saying clever things to other clever people. This devotion to the intellect left her very little time to do the cleaning or check whether the milk had gone off. Soon Alice was busy about the place being Gertrude's cook, secretary, editor and, presumably when she wasn't too tired, her lover.

Wives in history so often get overlooked. It is a little known fact that Karl Marx would never have written *Das Kapital* if his wife, Jenny, hadn't been fed up with their own lack of Kapital and not being able to feed the kids. Alice was in effect Gertrude's wife and enabled her to be brilliant at all hours. As Alice once said of a successful night of salon chatter – "*This has been a most wonderful evening. Gertrude has said things tonight it will take her ten years to understand.*"

Gertrude's life in Paris was full of creativity and critique which left Alice getting the croissants in and entertaining the wives of great men who came to call. Indeed had she written her own memoirs she intended to call the book *Wives of Geniuses I Have Sat With*. It wasn't all fun. Picasso may have thought his lover, Fernande Olivier, was worth painting sixty times but according to Alice she was "*not at all amusing*".

Gertrude's intelligence didn't stop her going through a less than attractive period when she thought Adolf Hitler was good for world peace. Despite this hiccup she and Alice nobly stayed in France during both world wars. World War One seems to have been their best war. Madame Matisse taught Alice to knit while her husband Henri banged on to Gertrude about being a wild beast of art. Even Gertrude must have got bored because eventually she ordered a truck from America and the two women spent the last two years of the war ferrying medical supplies about the place in the name of The American Fund for French Wounded. They named the truck Auntie after Gertrude's aunt Pauline, "*who always behaved admirably in emergencies and behaved fairly well most times if she was flattered*".

Although it would be many years before The Village People would make being gay something to sing about, Gertrude was the first person to use the word 'gay' to refer to her same-sex inclination. Indeed, in her story *Miss Furr*

& Miss Skeene, published in 1922, she used the expression a hundred times until it possibly became a tad tiresome. *"They were . . . gay, they learned little things that are things in being gay . . . they were quite regularly gay."*

They were also, quite possibly, regularly stoned. After Gertrude passed away to the great salon in the sky Alice published her own literary memoir under the title *The Alice B. Toklas Cookbook*. The artist Brion Gysin provided her with a recipe for 'Haschich Fudge', which he described as *"an entertaining refreshment for a Ladies' Bridge Club or a chapter meeting of the DAR"*. The DAR or Daughters of the American Revolution is an American women's group of eye-watering conservatism who might well have been enlivened by the mix of fruit, nuts, spices . . . and cannabis. Today Alice is remembered for her enlivening cakes and indeed some say that the slang term 'toke', meaning to inhale marijuana, is derived from her last name.

Alice and Gertrude parted in 1946 but only because Gertrude died. Alice carried on gamely writing recipes until she passed away in poverty, aged eighty-nine. She is buried next to her beloved in the Père Lachaise Cemetery in Paris. In keeping with a life dedicated to supporting her partner, Alice's name is engraved on the back of Stein's headstone.

Emily Post

1872—1960

Emily Post was the doyenne of American Etiquette, a title which some Europeans might have the poor manners to suspect of not being hotly contested. Emily was awash with good manners. There was nothing she didn't know about tea gowns or the rather complex rules governing which kind of 'elevators' require a man to take his hat off, or indeed, the answer to this rather vexing question: should damask be hemmed or hem stitched? (Hemmed by hand, of course. I'm surprised you had to ask.)

Emily began her journey towards social grace from the beginning by not being clear about her birthday. She may have been born on October 27, 1872 but it could just as easily have been October 3, 27 or 30, 1873. It is not a subject upon which a woman of breeding should dwell. Emily also knew enough about etiquette to realise that it is easier to know how to arrange all the cutlery for any event if you are born with a silver spoon in your mouth in the first place.

She was born into a wealthy socialite family in Baltimore, Maryland and led a heady life of chaperones and cotillions. ('Cotillion' is a marvellous and underrated word which may not have been fully understood by society. It's the old French word for petticoat yet the Americans used it to describe a social dance where showing your underwear would not go well.) Educated at home, Emily was then polished off at Miss Graham's finishing school in New York. She married a society banker, Edwin Main Post. Sadly, Edwin liked

The Limes
The Avenue
Dayton
Ohio

June 5th 1938

Dear Miss Post,

My husband and I have o__ __mained
for three months. My husband ___ ___ for our
first dinner party. I do_ ___ __se
the fish knives wh___ ___
my mother-in-law ___
However, I would be so___
do you think it con___
I am so terribly an___
and I am afraid th___
not offend her.

Yours Sincerely

J. M. E___

society rather too much and they divorced after he 'banked' in the wrong places. Finding herself financially embarrassed Emily began writing a book to prevent embarrassment of all kinds.

In 1922 she published *Etiquette – The Blue Book of Social Usage*, a book to help the nouveau riche, and became pleasingly riche herself. The publication went on to hold the distinction of being second only to the Bible as the book most often not returned or stolen from libraries. Clearly people read her work but didn't entirely follow the rules. In 1945 USO clubs for American troops reported Emily Post as the most requested book after the *Rand McNally Atlas*. This suggests many soldiers didn't know where they were going or what to say when they got there.

The Blue Book in a nutshell

1. Be nice to others.

2. Don't go on overnight automobile trips with a man.

3. Never wear light stockings on a heavy ankle.

4. Remember – a woman is ready to meet most emergencies
if she has a hair-pin and a visiting card.

The book went through many editions and endless reprints but good manners forbid me to tell you how much money she made. It seems that people right across America were desperate for advice, so she also had a radio show and a daily column on good taste syndicated in more than 200 newspapers which generated a weekly postbag of over 5,000 letters.

'Etiquette' come from the French, *étiquette*, and literally means a label. It started because the royal court of King Louis XIV were worryingly idle. The French nobles were so busy being noble that they didn't have jobs. The King needed to give them something to do so that no one would start thinking revolution was a good idea. Louis devised elaborate social customs which he wrote down on small tickets. The rules were very picky and you could tell who took them seriously by the length of the smallest finger on their left hand. No one was allowed to knock on the King's door. Instead, they had to gently scratch on the door with their left little finger until given permission to enter. Those who wanted to show off their devotion to this rule grew that fingernail longer than the others.

The word 'etiquette' first appeared in the English language around 1750. It's hard to know what triggered the introduction. The year before John Cleland wrote *Fanny Hill (Memoirs of a Woman of Pleasure)* while languishing in a debtors' prison. The very suggestion of women having pleasure is just the thing to prompt talk about good manners.

The Emily Post Institute now has an Online Etiquette Encyclopaedia called *Etipedia*® where you can learn perfectly sensible modern manners such as never tweeting about what you had for breakfast.

The *Chicago News* reported "*While Betty Grable is the Army's Pin Up Girl, Emily Post is their Look Up Girl.*"

Elizabeth Woodville

1437—1492

Eᴌɪᴢᴀʙᴇᴛʜ ᴡᴀs ʙᴏʀɴ ɪɴ 1437 to a noble family who were good at most things apart from spelling. Today we write Woodville but in her own time anything from Wydeville to Widvile would have been entirely fine, suggesting a pleasing medieval disinterest in identity theft.

Elizabeth was said to be the most beautiful woman in Britain, with *"heavy-lidded eyes like those of a dragon"* – not a compliment you hear much these days. When she was around about nineteen she married Sir John Grey of Groby, a Lancastrian, who history books say 'fell at St. Albans' in 1461. Many have fallen at St Albans during parky weather but, sadly, John was killed in battle and left Elizabeth with two sons. By now Edward IV, a Yorkist, was King of England (hold on tight as we race through some parts of history). As a Lancastrian Elizabeth was on the other side of a dispute over the correct colour for roses which had managed to rage with the Yorkists for about 100 years. Liz, however, was bold. She wanted land for her sons so she went to see King Ed and, after one of those romantic meetings in the woods you normally only get in films, she and the King plighted their troth and married secretly.

It's fair to say no one was pleased and things got worse when Elizabeth, who I think has been dead long enough for me to get away with calling her greedy and unscrupulous, kept getting the King to give land and money to her relations. Liz and Ed had ten kids of whom the 'Princes in the Tower', Edward V and his brother, Richard, did least well. When Liz's husband Edward IV died a heady game of numbers followed where, trust me, I can only scratch the surface. Ed V was only twelve so his uncle Richard of Gloucester (the hunchback one in Shakespeare) took the throne as Richard III, imprisoning Ed V and young Richard. Richard III then demanded that Elizabeth also turn over to his custody her daughters so she did. Eventually Richard III was killed by Henry Tudor (Bosworth Field but there isn't the time). Henry became Henry VII and married Elizabeth's daughter (also annoyingly called Elizabeth) who followed in the family business and became Queen. The Princes were probably murdered in the tower and Elizabeth Woodville retired to a nunnery where she had plenty of time to consider her failure to win *Mother of the Year*.

Elizabeth spent her final years in Bermondsey Abbey in Southwark near the Tower of London. It was a Benedictine monastery which means that at least the after-dinner liqueurs were pleasant. Southwark wasn't all piety. Local prostitutes were known as 'Winchester Geese' because the local Bishop, the Bishop of Winchester, took rent from the brothels round his palace. Always good to see the church doing what they can for the community. She died there in June 1492 aged fifty-five.

Britain, rather like American television, has had a series of dynasties. Elizabeth was part of the House of York which gave way to the Tudors who were followed by the Stuarts. Eventually everyone gave up on the whole idea of a British-bred monarchy and new royals had to be imported from Germany.

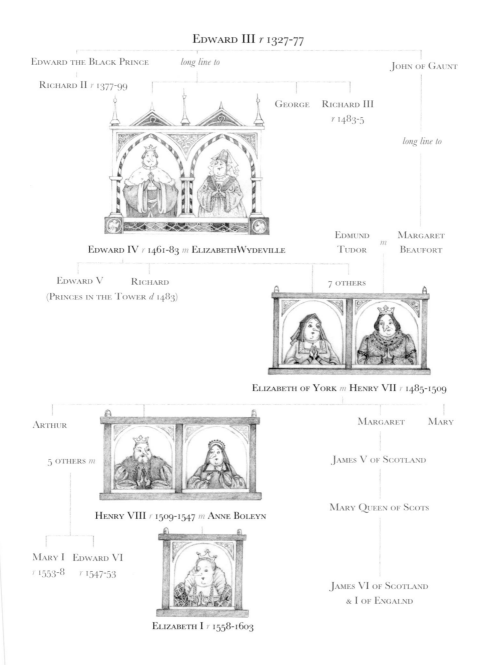

EDWARD III *r* 1327-77

EDWARD THE BLACK PRINCE   *long line to*   JOHN OF GAUNT

RICHARD II *r* 1377-99

GEORGE   RICHARD III
r 1483-5

long line to

EDMUND   MARGARET
TUDOR *m* BEAUFORT

EDWARD IV *r* 1461-83 *m* ELIZABETH WYDEVILLE

EDWARD V   RICHARD   7 OTHERS

(PRINCES IN THE TOWER *d* 1483)

ELIZABETH OF YORK *m* HENRY VII *r* 1485-1509

ARTHUR   MARGARET   MARY

5 OTHERS *m*   JAMES V OF SCOTLAND

HENRY VIII *r* 1509-1547 *m* ANNE BOLEYN

MARY QUEEN OF SCOTS

MARY I   EDWARD VI
r 1553-8   *r* 1547-53

JAMES VI OF SCOTLAND
& I OF ENGALND

ELIZABETH I *r* 1558-1603

Dame Ethel Smyth

1858–1944

Have you heard of her? Probably not. Should you have? Absolutely. She was a fabulous composer to whom George Bernard Shaw once wrote "*It was your music that cured me for ever of the old delusion that women could not do man's work in art and all other things . . . your Mass (in D) will stand up in the biggest company! Magnificent!*" She was famous in her own time ($4/4$ and $3/4$) partly because she was eccentric, often conducting (especially at winter afternoon concerts) in tweeds and never being the least bit interested in whether her hat was on straight. So – great with a tune, less clever at fashion.

Dame Ethel's dad was a General (J. H. Smyth) while her mum Nina was not. Ethel was born on April 23, 1858. Everyone argues about exactly where she came into the world but it might have been in Sidcup, Kent. This would be good for Sidcup as it might be the most famous thing about the place. From her earliest years Ethel appalled her father by wanting to study music. General Smyth was having none of it so the teenaged Ethel went on strike. Like all youthful protest this mainly consisted of locking herself in her room. Unlike any similar protest of teenagers today it ended by her father allowing her, aged nineteen, to go to Leipzig to study.

Leipzig has the world's largest facilities for primates but Ethel ignored this and instead made friends with Grieg, Tchaikovsky, Dvorák, Joachim, Clara Schumann and Brahms, all of whom she was able to name-drop later in life. Having had a taste of sorting her own life out Ethel returned to England where

she joined the militant suffragist movement and wrote 'March of the Women', the rallying theme of the suffragettes. She was a vigorous supporter of the movement, so vigorous in fact that she served two months in Holloway prison for throwing stones at a Conservative politician's windows. The legendary conductor Sir Thomas Beecham visited her in prison and wrote "*I arrived in the main courtyard of the prison to find the noble company of martyrs marching round it and singing lustily their war-chant ('March of the Women') while the composer, beaming approbation from an overlooking upper window, beat time in almost Bacchic frenzy with a toothbrush.*"

Smyth never married but . . . how can I put this in way that wouldn't have upset her? . . . she had many 'devoted friendships' with famous and infamous folk like Emmeline Pankhurst, Edith Somerville and Virginia Woolf. Bearing that in mind it won't surprise anyone that she was a sporty girl – a keen rider and, before anyone thought it a good idea for women, terribly fond of mountaineering, cycling and golf.

She was made Dame of the British Empire in 1922, was the very first woman to receive an honorary degree from Oxford University and the first female composer to have her work performed at the Metropolitan Opera in New York. She died on May 8, 1944 and her obituary in *The Times* quoted a friend as saying "*I cherish a picture of*

her, sitting bolt upright in the corner of a first-class carriage between Surbiton and Woking; she was armed with a great bundle of weeklies, which she examined rapidly, crumpled into balls, and hurled recklessly aside with snorts of disapproval, while the rest of the compartment submitted meekly to this astonishing bombardment." Glorious.

Tchaikovsky was complimentary in his diary about Ethel. He said she was *"one of the few women composers whom one can seriously consider to be achieving something valuable in the field of musical creation"*. He also said that *". . . no English-woman can be without her peculiarities and eccentricities"* and that Ethel's included her devotion to her dog Marco, her passion for hunting and *"her incredible, incomprehensible veneration, nay, passion for the enigmatic musical genius of Brahms."*

Marco was a half-breed St Bernard famous for always being at Ethel's side but never entirely in her control. He once nearly ruined a rehearsal at the house of celebrated Russian violinist Adolph Brodsky by knocking over the cellist's desk. It says something about Tchaikovsky (but heaven knows what) that he bracketed a passion for St Bernards and Brahms in the same category of eccentricity.

Dame Ethel interviewed on the subject of fame:

"Because I have conducted my own operas and love sheep-dogs; because I generally dress in tweeds, and sometimes, at winter afternoon concerts, have even conducted in them; because I was a militant suffragette and seized a chance of beating time to *"The March of the Women"* from the window of my cell in Holloway Prison with a tooth-brush; because I have written books, spoken speeches, broadcast, and don't always make sure that my hat is on straight; for these and other equally pertinent reasons, in a certain sense I am well known."

Courtesans

T IME FOR A BIT OF SEX so here is a woman with big jugs, sorry, big jug. The word 'courtesan' hasn't done well over the years. It came from the Italian *cortigiano* which just meant a woman who hung about at court. The world being what it is it wasn't long before female courtiers were thought to be hanging about for the wrong reasons. After that it was a quick downhill slide to them being seen as ladies whose favours could be bought. There have been many celebrated courtesans such as . . .

Thaïs

THE GREEKS DIDN'T SPEAK ITALIAN so they called courtesans '*hetaera*'. We don't know a lot about Thaïs' childhood except that she was from Athens and when she grew up she liked to hang out with Alexander the Great. There is more tittle-tattle about her adulthood because long after her death more than 2,300 years ago, we still know that she was a bit of a party girl. In 330BC Alexander and his gang were having a drinking party outside the palace of Persepolis in what we call Iran and what they called the capital of the Achaemenid Empire. It was quite the festive occasion with female musicians keeping everyone cheery. Alcohol can always get out of hand and after a few sherries, Thaïs gave a speech in which she persuaded Al that what they really wanted to do was to burn down the palace. Everyone grabbed a blazing torch and headed off led by a phalanx of female flautists. Because Alexander was great he threw his torch first but Thaïs was next and soon the palace had no resale value.

It's hard to say whether Thaïs was Alexander's lover or just a Persepolis-burning kind of pal. After he died she had three kids with Ptolemy, who became King of Egypt. It seems unlikely that they married because he had other wives – first Eurydice and then Berenice, names which you rarely hear called out in the modern playground.

Barbara Palmer, 1ˢᵗ Duchess of Cleveland, 1640–1709

Babs did well as a courtesan. She had five kids with Charles II and became known to some as 'The Uncrowned Queen' and to others as the 'curse of the nation'. She would have been fantastic fodder for modern gossip magazines for she was the perfect mix of extravagance, bad temper and promiscuity.

Her childhood was not easy. Her dad died in 1643 fighting for the Royalists in the English Civil War. Six years later King Charles I lost his head and her poor family had to keep so quiet about being on the King's side that every year they celebrated Charles' son's birthday by climbing down into the cellar and toasting his health in the dark. Meanwhile Boy Charles was wandering about Europe in a curious sort of extended royal gap year.

Barbara was beautiful but no one was keen to snap her up on the marriage market because she had no money. In the end she married Roger Palmer who became both the 1ˢᵗ Earl of Castlemaine and miserable. Roger and Babs sailed to see Charles in The Hague to get him to come home. Charles was very grateful. He gave Roger a title and rogered his wife. Poor Roger Palmer was now out of the picture and soon Barbara was so important she was able to give birth to her second child at Hampton Court Palace while the King and his new wife were honeymooning.

Over the years her influence with the King came and went but she carried on helping herself to money from the Privy Purse and taking bribes from anyone who wanted to give them. When Charles died she was forty-five and not at all ready to retire. She went on to have another affair and child with an actor known as Cardonell "Scum" Goodman, who promptly tried to poison her existing sons. When Roger died she married Major-General Robert "Beau" Fielding, whom she later had prosecuted for bigamy.

She died from dropsy aged sixty-eight at Chiswick Mall, which is a place in London and not an early shopping centre. Among her descendents are Diana, Princess of Wales and Sir Anthony Eden.

Laura Bell, 1829–1894

LAURA WAS A FAMOUS COURTESAN of Victorian England, not an era in which one would imagine the courtesan business might flourish. She would eventually grow up to be Mrs Thistlethwayte and a moral evangelist but before then she managed to get about a bit.

Laura was born at Glenavy, Co. Antrim. Her father was either a bailiff on the Irish Estates of the Marquis of Hertford or he may have been the actual Marquis of Hertford. No one was prepared to say then and hardly anyone has a view now. Laura got a job as a shop girl in Belfast. It can't have been cheery as she worked in the 'Mourning Department'. The wages were poor but as compensation Laura discovered that men will sometimes pay for a little 'service on the side'. Even Oscar Wilde's father, the doctor and antiquarian William Wilde, was said to have been what can only be described as a 'keen customer'.

Laura moved to London. She got a job at Jay's General Mourning House in Regent Street but, determined not to be gloomy, she bought a carriage drawn by two white horses. Every day she drove about Hyde Park accompanied by a young 'tiger' of a servant dressed in "*a waist coat of black and yellow stripes and a tall cockaded hat*". One day in 1850 Jung Bahadoor Rana, future ruler of Nepal, was in London and realised he needed something black. He popped into Jay's General Mourning House and fell head over heels for Laura. Pretty soon she had a very nice house in Belgravia and quite a lot of jewellery. Poor Jung went back home three months later leaving Laura £250,000 richer.

Eventually Laura married Captain August Frederick Thistlethwayte. It didn't go all that well. Laura loved to spend money and August was forever having to publish notices in the press saying he couldn't be responsible for his wife's debts. August died in a curious manner. Instead of summoning his valet with a bell he liked to fire his revolver into the ceiling. On August 9, 1887, he was found shot in his bedroom and it was assumed that he had accidentally shot himself while attempting to summon the valet.

Laura was a rich widow with nothing to do so she converted herself into an evangelical preacher and started bothering people about their morals. She became great friends with the Prime Minister William Gladstone, who always had a soft spot for ladies of the night. She died in 1894 and you can find her finally sleeping alone in Paddington Green Cemetery in London.

A footnote on her short time with the ruler of Nepal – Allegedly the British government were so delighted with this warming of British–Nepal relations via his relationship with Laura that they reimbursed Jung all the money he had lavished on her. For his part he never forgot her and was left with a determination to stay on the British side. To this day the relationship of the Nepalese Gurkha regiments with the British Army may have something to do with the particular skills of a golden-haired girl from Ireland.

POPE JOAN

Pope Joan

853—855 AD

POPE JOAN IS A RATHER clear figure in history – either she was the only woman ever to be Pope or some anti-Pope person made up a load of Papal bull. Thus her title was either Bishop of Rome, Vicar of Jesus Christ, Successor of the Prince of the Apostles, Supreme Pontiff of the Universal Church, Patriarch of the West, Primate of Italy, Sovereign of the State of the Vatican City, Archbishop and Metropolitan of the Roman Province, Servant of the Servants of God or she didn't have one.

As she may have been made up we can be a little cavalier with the facts. Obviously she would need to live in Rome (the Vatican has rarely moved house) but exactly when is unclear. This not surprising because it was most likely in the ninth century which was also known as the Very Dark Ages when hardly anything was clear.

Fact or fiction she is quite a girl. If she did exist then she was the only Pope to wreck a Vatican ceremony by giving birth. If she was a legend then she was strong enough a story for someone to spend a lot of seventeenth-century man hours shredding references to her in history books.

If Joan existed then she was probably originally called Agnes or possibly Gilberta or maybe Jutta (OK, I'm not sure) when she was born in Germany of English missionary parents. Annoyingly for a girl in the ninth century she was very bright which was, of course, unnatural and dangerous. This was a girl who wanted to break the glass ceiling before most people had glass. They say (you will note I am starting to get vague here) that at the age of twelve she was taken in 'masculine attire' to Athens by a 'learned man', a monk described as her teacher and lover which even today is deemed a poor combination.

Anyway, she was very clever and Martin of Troppau (who was Polish and wrote the history of the world in the ninth century, which must have taken less time than it would now) wrote that "*there was nobody equal to her*" when it came to studying science. Eventually, her knowledge of the scriptures led to her election as Pope John Anglicus where old Martin reckons she ruled for two years, seven months and four days before giving the game away by giving birth on the *Via Sacra* during a Papal procession.

According to most versions, tourists and passers-by were somewhat surprised when Pope John Anglicus tried to mount a horse, went into labour and gave birth to a son.

At this point one of two things happened –

The crowd tied her feet to the horse's tail, and stoned her to death.

or

She was banished to a convent where her son grew up to follow in the family business and become a bishop.

The case for Pope Joan having existed includes the fact that there used to be a statue of Joan alongside all the other Popes in the Cathedral of Siena until Pope Clement VIII commanded the sculpture be 'metamorphosed' into Pope Zacharias. The Church also brought in the 'chair exam' after her supposed reign, which compelled each newly elected Pope to sit naked on a chair with a hole in the middle while others had a look and declared *"Mas nobis nominus est"* – *"Our nominee is a man."* This was surely an embarrassing addition to an otherwise joyous day.

The case against is . . . uhm . . . there are no tea towels for sale with her face on in St Peter's Square.

The chair with the hole in the centre of the seat was called the *Sedes Stercoraria*. The existence of such chairs is not disputed but their purpose is debated. Some think they were either bidets or imperial birthing stools. The latter is the most likely as there is nothing a woman in labour likes better than having to aim the baby through a hole in a wooden throne.

Lady Eastnor

1827—1910

SOME WOMEN ARE DELIGHTFUL WHEN they are alive. Some, sadly, are a joy only when they've passed on. To be entrancing both dead and alive is a rare feat and part of what makes '*The Delectable Lady Eastnor*' entirely delectable. Her tale is not a totally happy narrative for it involves death, alcohol and an explosion but it is a story that may make you smile involving, as it does, death, alcohol and an explosion.

Lovely Lady Eastnor was born Virginia Pattle in Calcutta on January 14, 1827. She was one of nine Pattle sisters, a number which is not even useful in families desperate for impromptu netball matches. All the girls were said to be great beauties apart from the third one, Julia Margaret (Cameron), who grew up to be a pioneering photographer and took pictures of pretty people instead.

Amidst this bevy of beauties Virginia was said to be the one who was "*So staggeringly good-looking that passers-by stopped dead in their tracks at the sight of her.*" Virginia got these killer genes from her parents, James Pattle, a rich civil servant in India, and his French wife, Adeline de l'Étang, whose father was said to have been Marie Antoinette's lover. (This story is full of such titillating side roads but sadly we haven't the time.)

I hate to speak ill of the dead but it was said that Virginia's dad, James, liked a drink. Indeed he died of the stuff while the family were all living in Calcutta. The family had been there so long Virginia's Hindustani was rather more fluent than her English. James' dying wish, except perhaps for another drink, was for his body to be returned to the UK. The year was 1845 and in those days a trip from India to England involved a long sea journey. In order to preserve Jim's body it was placed pleasingly, rather appropriately, in a barrel of rum and put in the cabin next to his widow for the sea voyage. According to that other grande dame, Ethel Smyth, " . . . *in the middle of the night there was a loud explosion; Adeline rushed into the room and found the cask had burst . . . and there was her husband half out of it! The shock sent her off her head then and there, poor thing, and she died raving.*"

Now the poor Pattles had two dead parents on their hands and still endless hours of boredom and bouillon at sea. You would think they might have thought again about the corpse-in-the-cask plan as it hadn't gone all that well the first time but Dame Ethel declares they tried it again and packed Papa back in yet more rum before setting off on a new boat down the Ganges. Apparently all the sailors knew was that the barrels contained drink. They put a hole in the side and got so drunk the rum ran out and caught fire, whereupon the vessel "*ran on a rock, blew up and drifted ashore just below Hooghly [West Bengal]*".

I'm sure we've all had rough travel journeys but that takes some beating. Virginia and her sister Sophia arrived in sunny England trying to explain, presumably in Hindustani, why they had two dead parents, one looking terribly surprised and the other rather scorched round the edges.

Five years later Virginia married Charles Somers Cocks. She must have been delighted he was also known as Viscount Eastnor or she would have been the Delectable Mrs Somers Cocks. They went to live in a big castle where no doubt she shuddered whenever a cruise brochure landed on the doormat.

Charles and Virginia had three daughters. The eldest, Isabel, is well worth noting. She married Lord Henry Somerset. They had a son but Henry found he preferred the company of men and so they didn't have any more. When Henry literally buggered off, Virginia fought for custody of their child. This scandal left hardly anyone speaking to her except the sick and needy who

Isabel started visiting. She soon realised the evils of drink, became temperance mad and opened one of the first rehab clinics in the UK. By 1913 she topped *London Evening News* poll as the person the readers would most like as the first female Prime Minister.

On a barrel-related note – the first person to survive going over Niagara Falls in a barrel was a woman called Annie Taylor. She did this on her 43rd birthday, October 24, 1901. After her successful plunge Annie declared, "If it was with my dying breath, I would caution anyone against attempting the feat . . . I would sooner walk up to the mouth of a cannon, knowing it was going to blow me to pieces than make another trip over the Fall."

Queen Elizabeth I

1533—1603

I'M SURE WE ALL THINK we know Elizabeth I. She's like a relative everyone grew up hearing stories about. She had red hair, sent Raleigh off to discover the bicycle and invented Shakespeare. I think she also taught Francis Drake to play bowls at the seaside but there isn't the time. Did you know, however, that she suffered from anthrophobia which is a fear of flowers? Roses in particular, actually. It's a curious choice of phobia when, given her family background, you would have thought she had greater things to quake at than a table centrepiece.

Elizabeth was born in 1533 in the Chamber of Virgins in Greenwich Palace, a room that would set the benchmark for her later dating career. Her father was King Henry VIII so things must have looked pretty cheerful at the start. Then, when she was two-and-a-half, her dad had her mum, Anne Boleyn, beheaded which is the classic sort of dysfunctional family event that any therapist would have a field day with. Elizabeth had an older half-sister called Mary. Either girl might have inherited their Dad's business but he went on to have a son called Edward and made him ruler instead.

When her dad died Liz was fourteen. She went to live with her stepmother, Catherine Parr, who soon had a new husband, Thomas Seymour. It seems

Tom, who was forty, liked Liz a bit too much and kept trying to tell her bedtime stories. In the end Liz was sent away and Tom was also beheaded. By now the future Queen was awash with abandonment issues, none of which really improved when her half brother, the new King Edward VI, died of tuberculosis. He tried to leave his throne to his dad's sister's granddaughter, Lady Jane Grey, but everyone thought it was all getting silly and crowned Elizabeth's sister Mary instead.

Sadly religion came between the sisters. Mary was a Catholic while Liz was Protestant. Mary believed everyone should go to Mass while Liz wanted to promote the Church of England which has less incense and more jumble sales. Protestants started being killed and Mary became known as Bloody Mary. Lots of people didn't want a Queen named after a cocktail. They cheered Liz instead so the Queen put her sister in the Tower of London and not just to enjoy the tourist bits. Eventually Mary died and Liz finally took over when she was twenty-five. (I'm having to be quick here because she lived for an age.)

Everyone wanted Elizabeth to get married. Unfortunately for her the man she loved, an old childhood friend, Lord Robert Dudley, was already married. When his wife died falling down the stairs everyone was a little suspicious and, like any good soap-opera story line, in the end Dudley married somebody else.

Elizabeth never did marry but that may be because she had more family trouble than you find in a weekend in Albert Square. Liz's cousin, also called Mary, had gone into the family ruling business and was Queen of Scotland. Her husband, Lord Darnley, died and lots of people thought he'd been murdered, especially when Mary married someone else a few weeks later. Soon she was in prison as well. More rebelling, more Catholics cross with Protestants until Liz finally followed the traditional family way of dealing with things and had Mary beheaded.

It went on like that for years with people losing their heads over a Queen who eventually lost her looks and her hair. I imagine her at the end ordering wigs and makeup by post and chopping the head off anyone sending greetings by Interflora.

Everyone associates Elizabeth with the Spanish Armada. This was a fleet of boats which the Spaniards called *Grande y Felicísima Armada* or *Armada Invencible* which means '*Great and Most Fortunate Navy*' and '*The Invincible Fleet*' which is a shame because, you know, well, it wasn't.

Women
with Attitude

Some women in history have been so fantastic that everyone later claimed they were simply fantastical.

Queen Vishpala (c. 7000 BC)

QUEEN VISHPALA IS ONE OF those women some people doubt existed perhaps because she was so feisty. You can find her written about in the splendid *Rigveda* which is an ancient Indian sacred collection of *Vedic Sanskrit* hymns. (If you haven't read them I think you can be forgiven as they were written a few thousand years ago and poetry trends are tricky to keep up with.) If Vishpala did once tread the earth then she did it with quite a thump.

Nine thousand years after her death she appears not only in the *Rigveda* but also in a treatise entitled *A Brief Review of the History of Amputations and Prostheses* by Earl E. Vaderwerker Jr, MD. According to the *Rigveda*, Vishpala was a cracking warrior queen. Sadly she lost her leg in a battle but rather than quit, she had a prosthetic leg made and got back on her horse. The leg was made of iron so she may have sat a little skew-whiff but nevertheless she carried on battling. Earl Jr says it's the first mention of a prosthetic limb in history.

Queen Sammuramat (REIGNED C. 811—792 BC)

SAMMURAMAT (OR *Semiramis* IF YOU'RE GREEK) was a sassy lady from Assyria (present day northern Iraq). If you like a bit of legend then you'll go with the idea that she was raised in the desert by doves and discovered by shepherds. We do know that she ruled Assyria for some time but women's history not being all that interesting to the men who write it down, the origins of her reign are disputed. According to the Greeks her first husband was a royal advisor named Menos. One day Menos was in the middle of a battle that wasn't going brilliantly. He sent for his wife and she won the battle by outflanking the enemy. The King, Ninus, thought she was the business and stole Sammuramat from Menos. Menos was less than pleased and killed himself.

Sammuramat became Queen and Ninus thought she was marvellous. He asked her if she wanted anything. She said she wanted to rule for a day. Ninus thought it would be a laugh, had her crowned and she promptly had him executed. Sammuramat ruled on her own for the next forty-two years during which time she busily expanded her portfolio by beating other people up. Despite her busy official life she still had time for a hobby and created the Hanging Gardens of Babylon.

Queen Zenobia (REIGNED C. 240—274 AD)

THERE ARE SO MANY EMPIRES which have come
and then gone. The Akkadian Empire, the
Babylonian Empire, the Holborn Empire
and of course, the Palmyrene Empire, in
what is now Syria. Zenobia was Queen
of the Palmyrene Empire back in the
third century AD. She got the job
by marrying the King, Septimius
Odaenathus, but eventually he,
rather annoyingly, got
himself assassinated.

With time on her hands (and golf not
having been invented yet) she decided she
needed a hobby. Like many women with their
property, she realised her own place wasn't big
enough and in 269 set about conquering Egypt. Leading her army and not
being overly sensitive to other people's cultures she also took Anatolia, Syria,
Palestine and Lebanon. The loss of Egypt made its Roman prefect very unhappy
so he tried to take the country back. Zenobia, who was not to be trifled with,
had him beheaded.

She carried on being top dog for another five years until at last the Romans
knocked her over. She was taken to Rome in golden shackles. There are
various versions of what happened next. The jolliest one is where the Romans
fell for her charms, released her and she made a marvellous new life for herself
as a prominent Roman socialite.

Hua Mulan (c. 4ᵀᴴ–5ᵀᴴ century ad)

SIGH. HERE IS ANOTHER FINE woman that historians can't believe was real. Of course she was real. Not only is there a splendid Chinese poem called "*The Ballad of Mulan*", there is also an excellent cartoon by Disney. The ballad is set in the Northern Wei dynasty (386–534) and tells the tale of Mulan's ageing Dad being conscripted into the Imperial Army. Her father is too sick to serve and so Mulan dresses up as a man and goes instead. Mulan the man is triumphant and so the Emperor offers her a job but the simple girl decides to go home to her family. Back at home her former army buddies visit and are amazed at the change in their old friend.

Tomoe Gozen (C. 1157—1247)

IF YOU'VE NOT HAD AS much time to devote to Japanese history as you had
hoped then you may not be all that familiar with the Genpei War which
began in 1180 and lasted for five years. Depending on your level of knowledge,
telling you that it was a conflict between the Taira and Minamoto clans
during the late-Heian period may not be all that helpful. What you should
know, however, is the story of the famously beautiful samurai warrior Tomoe
Gozen who fought in it.

Tomoe was a Japanese legend with brilliant sword and bow skills and an
ability to break wild horses that left every equine shivering. She fought for the
Minamotos and helped capture Kyoto which could've been the beginning of
a great limerick but sadly no one thought of it at the time.

Again there are various endings
to the warrior woman's life.

1. She was captured by the
enemy and got married.

2. She became a nun.

3. She fled the battlefield clutching
an enemy's head and was never
seen again.

Tough choice.

Cicely Mary Hamilton

1872—1952

CICELY WAS A CELEBRATED ACTRESS, suffragist and feminist. All perfectly splendid things today, but sadly she was born in 1872 and grew up during a time when these particular occupations were unlikely to amuse anyone, particularly the Queen. Our heroine did not have the happiest of childhoods. For little Cicely this was a good thing as she also grew up to be a

writer and there is little more beneficial to the professional scribbler than a dysfunctional upbringing. She was born in Paddington, London but sadly I have no further details and so am going to presume it was at home and not whilst waiting for a train.

Cicely began life as Cicely Hammill, daughter of a Captain in the Gordon Highlanders (who revelled in the name of Danzil) and a mother (Maude)

who may have been less than stable. Fairly swiftly Pater went off to Egypt, Mater went off to an asylum and Cicely was landed with foster parents. She finished her education and, with no parents to warn her against it, proceeded down a route many Victorian girls knew to be naughty – she took to the stage.

Cicely joined the repertory company of Edmund Tearle. Edmund was a professional 'tragedian' who prided himself on being able to keep the whole of Shakespeare in his head. Indeed the company once famously did eight (including Saturday matinée) different Shakespeare plays at Blyth Theatre Royal in a single week. For ten years Cicely toured the country playing parts such as Gertrude in *Hamlet*, Emilia in *Othello* and one of the witches in *Macbeth*. The latter role was probably a fairly clear clue that she wasn't really leading lady material, so she started writing plays instead.

Her work was a huge success, particularly the play *Diana of Dobsons* which was produced in the West End by one of London's first actress-managers, the suffragette Lena Ashwell. In their spare time Lena and Cicely campaigned away for women to be allowed to vote with Cicely joining our other great woman of history, the composer Ethel Smyth (you remember . . . do pay attention) to write 'The March of the Women'.

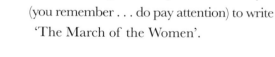

When World War One rumbled into view Cicely wanted to do her bit. She joined the Scottish Women's Hospital Unit and in 1916 helped nurse soldiers wounded at the Battle of the Somme. In three days

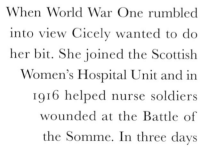

her unit treated 300 new patients and yet Cicely was champing at the bit. Despite her skill with a triangular bandage she knew there would be nothing better for the men in the trenches than a bit of Shakespeare.

As if it were the most natural thing in the world Cicely and Lena Ashwell formed a repertory company that toured the Western Front. It was not easy. As Cicely herself explained "*The leading lady will wrestle with the mechanism of a refractory curtain while the acting manager collects the properties and the comedian knocks in nails.*" The shows were a trial as leading men were usually drawn from the ranks and were often called away just before the curtain went up or only had costumes available in khaki colour. The company were instructed ". . . *owing to the limited dimensions of the stage, the presence of unnecessary furniture is not encouraged . . . only in cases of extreme urgency is an extra armchair permitted.*"

Cicely was a wonderful writer and her novels remain a gripping read. She concluded her life as a journalist campaigning for free birth-control advice for women. All great stuff but I shall always see her dressed in her finest on a makeshift stage spouting Shakespeare while all around her war raged.

In 1931 Cicely took to writing travel books. She started with *Modern Germanies as seen by an Englishwoman*. Clearly feeling she was on a roll, the following year she published *Modern Italy as seen by an Englishwoman* then *Modern France as seen by* . . . etc. It went on like that as she traipsed about the modern world being a woman and English. Finally she wrote a book about modern Sweden and gave up.

Matilda of Flanders

1031—1083

ATILDA OF FLANDERS WAS KNOWN to the French as *Mathilde de Flandre* and to the Dutch as *Mathilda van Vlaanderen*, all of which seems to show that everyone knew she was called Matilda and that she came from Flanders. The devil, however, is in the detail for quite a lot of it is on the hazy side. Matilda did come from Flanders but it is possible her family called her Maud. Whatever they called her no one seems to have bothered to remember her birthday so all we know is that she was born about 1031. Maud was probably the shortest Queen of England of all time. I say probably, because they measured her long after she was dead. She was somewhere between four foot two inches and five foot which just shows how notoriously difficult bones are to assess. What does seem clear, however, is that she was a bit of a madam.

Her whole family were posh enough to give each other endless presents with royal crests on. Her mum was Adèle of France, daughter of Robert II of France and her dad was Baldwin V, Count of Flanders. This luscious lineage made Matilda a good catch and she caught the attention of her cousin, William the Conqueror. Before he started conquering Will was known to his face as plain Duke William II of Normandy and, presumably behind his back, William the Bastard. The latter moniker had nothing to do with his personality but due to being born the wrong side of the blanket. Will decided to marry Matilda but because he was a busy man he sent a friend to ask. This is the kind of proposal that rarely goes well with a girl and Matilda's reply was

not entirely polite. She told the chum that she was far to posh to even think of marrying a bastard. There are several versions of what happened next.

Possibly Will rode to Bruges where Matilda was on her way to church, grabbed her long braids to pull her off her horse into the street and rode off. Or he rode to her father's house in Lille, pulled her long braids so she fell on the ground and then beat her. Either way it wasn't pleasant, it definitely involved long braids and it worked a treat because Maud married him. Not everyone was keen on the match. The Pope tried to ban the marriage on the grounds of 'consanguinity' which is an ancient rule that says marrying your cousin is just too confusing at family events. Will and Maud talked the Pope round this little problem by promising to build an abbey called *l'Abbaye aux Dames* in Caen which apparently is all it takes to get round the restrictions about swimming in a very shallow gene pool.

The marriage doesn't seem to have been a total love fest. Matilda did buy her groom a perfectly nice ship to invade England with (a gift rarely seen on a wedding list) but after he conquered England and became King it took her more than a year to visit.

Matilda may not have been the world's cuddliest Queen. Rumour has it that she had once been in love with an English ambassador called Brihtric, who failed to return her favours. Years later when William was off conquering elsewhere and she was in charge of England, she used her power to confiscate Brihtric's lands and chuck him in jail where he died. Sadly he failed to take note of the warning that "*Heaven has no rage like love to hatred turned, Nor hell a fury like a woman scorned*" mainly because Shakespeare wouldn't be born for another five centuries to whom it would then be wrongly attributed.

Matilda had nine, possibly ten, kids with William. One daughter is a bit dubious and we all know families like that. Between breast feeds she may have had time to take up embroidery. Lots of people used to think she threaded a needle for the *Bayeux Tapestry*. They thought this because the French called it *La Tapisserie de la Reine Mathilde*. It turns out this was wrong as indeed was calling it a tapestry at all. It's an embroidery, was probably made in Kent and she had nothing to do with it. There is much in history Matilda had nothing to do with, including a musical that bears her name.

Matilda can't have been the greatest Queen of England because she concluded her life living back in France. In fact she went to live in Normandy without William in the very abbey she had built in order to get married in the first place. If you fancied looking her up now that is also where she is buried. Despite living in separate countries William seems to have liked being married to Matilda. She died aged fifty-one and he expressed his grief in two ways:

1. He became tyrannical

2. He gave up hunting.

Neither method is recommended today by grief counsellors.

More than a thousand years later Matilda continues to hold the record for being England's shortest Queen, which is something . . . probably.

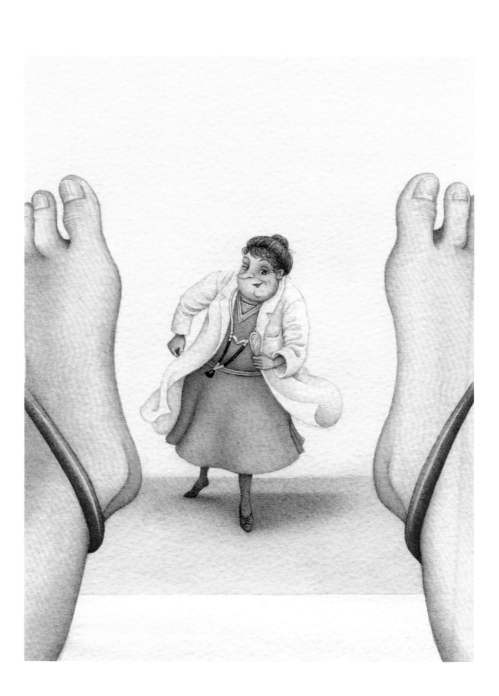

Marie Stopes

1880—1958

MARIE STOPES WAS A PROPER mix of the old and the new. She was a palaeobotanist which meant she liked plants that were very very ancient and she founded the first birth control clinic in the British Empire which at the time was very very modern. Pleasingly one can unite these two rather disparate interests through the *Kahun Gynaecological Papyrus*. The *Kahun* doesn't feature in many book clubs but it was written around 1800 BCE and is the oldest medical text of any kind. It deals with women's 'issues' and if you take your time to scroll through it you could learn how to make a contraceptive out of that ancient plant the acacia tree.

Acacia gum, it transpires, is a natural spermicide. (The gum was also used in mummification which is another more permanent method of birth control.) The papyrus was packed with baby limiting advice including smearing the 'mouth of the womb' with a mix of honey and sodium carbonate and that all time favourite, a pessary made from crocodile dung which would put most people off their sexual stride.

Reducing the number of babies women have is clearly a long standing concern but nevertheless it wasn't a natural topic for a Victorian woman. Marie was born in Edinburgh in 1880 of rather corking parents – her dad was a brewer and a palaeontologist (still old stuff but more bones than plants) while her mum was a scholar and a suffragette. Her parents met at a meeting of the British Association for the Advancement of Science. Presumably they carried on banging on about science until Marie grew up, gave in and went to study it herself.

She clearly loved her subject although some of it seems a little dry including the entirely dried up Ebbsfleet River where Marie dug about looking for a Ph.D. Soon she was lecturing all and sundry about old, dry plants, pushing boundaries and in 1904 becoming the first female academic at the University of Manchester. She still wasn't exactly the talk of the town unless the town wanted to spend time discussing coal mines and seed ferns.

Even Marie knew she needed to get a bit more of a life. In 1910 she headed off to somewhere geological called the Fern Ledges which lie or stand or whatever geological things do in New Brunswick, Canada. She met a man called Reginald Ruggles Gates, two days later they got engaged and a few weeks later were married.

All did not go well and soon they were getting divorced with Marie citing lack of consummation as her main reason. In 1915 Marie began writing a book called *Married Love* about how marriage ought to work and she included a chapter on contraception. The publisher Walter Blackie wrote to her – "*Pray excuse the suggestion, but don't you think you should wait publication until after the war, at least? There will be few enough men for the girls to marry: and a book would frighten off the few.*"

Marie carried on dating and met a man called Humphrey Verdon Roe who was everything any woman could desire – a wealthy manufacturing magnate. Roe helped her get the book published and it was an instant success. People started writing to her saying she was either a saint or the devil incarnate. Stopes married Roe and started practising what she had preached. Interrupted by the odd court case and tickings off from the Catholic Church Marie and Roe ploughed on and in 1921 opened the Mothers' Clinic in North London which offered birth control advice. Today the Marie Stopes International organisation operates in over forty countries with 452 clinics worldwide.

Marie also wrote plays and poetry, which is nice, and advocated eugenics, which was less good. She wrote that *"the inferior, the depraved, and the feeble-minded"* ought to be compulsorily sterilised and when her son Harry married a woman who was myopic she cut him out of her will on the grounds that grandchildren might inherit the condition. In 1936 Marie also wrote a letter to Hitler sending him some love poems to distribute to German youth. She lived to regret this generous gesture as Hitler later was less than charming and had all her books burnt.

Marie and her husband had a contract allowing them 'free love' within their marriage. She believed people should express themselves sexually unless, of course, they were homosexual in which case they should stay home and take up tapestry.

A children's rhyme of the time bears repeating –

> *Jeanie, Jeanie, full of hopes,*
> *Read a book by Marie Stopes,*
> *But, to judge from her condition,*
> *She must have read the wrong edition.*

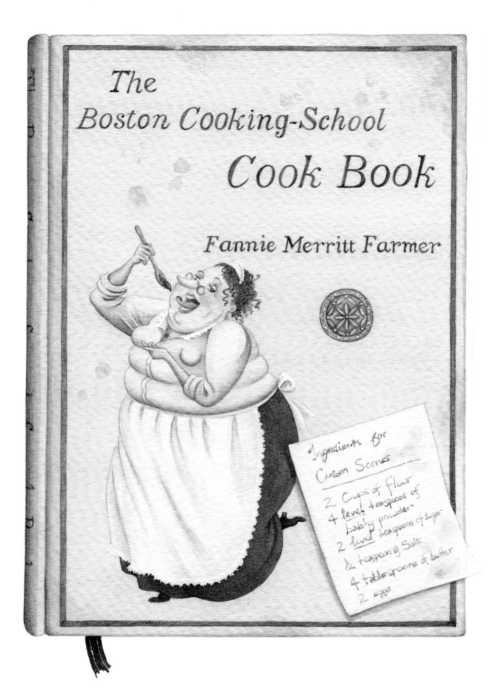

Fannie Farmer

1857—1915

THE NAME FANNIE OR FANNY has a long association with food. There was the British television star Fanny Craddock who liked to cook and there was the American comedienne Fanny Brice who loved to cook but of all the famous food Fannies, first was Fannie Merritt Farmer. Our Fannie of the Day was born in 1857 in Medford, Massachusetts in the United States. She once said that *"Progress in civilization has been accompanied by progress in cookery."* There are those that would argue that no one knew how to stuff a dormouse like the Romans but you know what she meant. Fortunately for her Fannie came from a town that was full of progress.

Amongst other things, Medford also spawned the song 'Jingle Bells', the world's first 'practical four-wheeled roller skate' (I do so loathe an impractical roller skate) and the scandal of the Gypsy Moths. In 1868, when Fannie was eleven, a French astronomer and naturalist, Léopold Trouvelot, living at 27 Myrtle Street in Medford, allowed several Gypsy Moths he was experimenting with to escape. They promptly ate all the plants in town and spread out across America.

I like to imagine Fannie as a young teenager wandering about humming a Christmas song while a moth bears off the last leaf in town. Sadly Fannie did not stroll for long. She was the eldest of four daughters born into a family which, unusual for the time, expected them all to go to college. When she was sixteen Fannie suffered a paralytic stroke that instead forced her to stay at

home convalescing. Fannie did what any sensible woman made to stay at home often resorts to – she started cooking. By the time she was thirty she had had quite a lot of practice and was thought to be quite good. Nevertheless a friend suggested she enrol in the Boston Cooking School.

So off Fannie went to learn far too much about what had been renamed 'domestic science' in order to make it seem like a more interesting occupation. She studied nutrition, diet, cooking for sick people, well people, small people and old people along with cleaning techniques for everyone as well as that beloved old chestnut 'household management'. Either Fannie was very good or the school wasn't great because within two years she had been made Principal and was running the place.

At the time most recipes were written with more than a hint of casualness. People were advised to use 'a piece of butter the size of an egg' or 'a teacup of milk'. Fannie thought that such instructions were far too vague and that all measurements ought to be far more exact. Today we call that 'obsessive-compulsive disorder'. She decided to write a cookbook of her own. Her tome was entitled *The Boston Cooking-School Cookbook*, and she started a cookbook trend by getting recipies from someone else's book
– *Mrs. Lincoln's Boston Cook Book.* Not everyone thought this was entirely marvellous as Fannie failed to print the key words 'Thank you, Mrs. Lincoln.' The book was popular because it contained

indispensable recipes for Fried Corn Meal Mush, Fried Hominy and details of what to do with Succotash. It was, however, mainly praised for being very modern.

Society was heading for a time when people had a lot less servants but no less need to eat.[*] The instructions in the book were concise and clear with Fannie (soon to be known by the coveted title of 'the mother of level measurements') carefully explaining just *how* level a level teaspoon ought to be. The publishers had had no faith in such a venture so Fannie paid the initial printing costs and retained the copyright and profits. Thus when the book went on to become one of the most popular American cookbooks of all time it made Fannie an extremely rich woman who, ironically, didn't have to cook if she didn't fancy it. She went on to write the even more gripping sequel *Food and Cookery for the Sick and Convalescent*. Fannie died aged fifty-seven still inventing new things to do with food and relentlessly checking everything was level.

---

[*] I had an English teacher who banged on about when to use 'fewer' and when to use 'less'. She was so obsessed that I take a perverse pride in getting it wrong. This does not reflect well on me and I should do it less or fewer.

Fanny Burney

1752—1840

HERE IS A FUNNY THING about fame. You may not have heard of Fanny Burney but no doubt you will know Jane Austen. (If you don't know Jane Austen then well done for being able to read this.) Fanny was a huge hit in her lifetime but is not so well known now. Jane, on the other hand, was not a roaring success when alive but a box office smash much later. If you love Jane then you should know Fanny for she inspired young Austen and indeed the title *Pride and Prejudice* was taken from one of Fanny's novels.

Fanny was born in 1752 in Lynn Regis in Norfolk. The place is now called King's Lynn which is much the same name but with less Latin. Both her parents were musicians with her father, Charles, being a very good organist. Fanny was the third of six children. She was a bookworm and either shy or simply desperate to get away from the noise of the other kids, and indeed the organ.

Eventually the Burneys realised there was more to do in London than in Norfolk and moved to the centre of town. Here their house was always full of theatrical types like the actor-manager David Garrick, who would pop in to show off. Sadly, when Fanny was ten her mother died. Charles then married a widow whom Fanny disliked. Unhappy and a teenager, Fanny began keeping a diary of her private thoughts. Soon she found this a marginally obsessive enteprise and, when she was twenty-six, she published a novel called *Evelina*, in which a young woman rises above the bad manners of her cousins and does

what she was born to do – marry a nobleman. The book was published anonymously because young women of the eighteenth century didn't want their reputations sullied by naughtiness like writing. It was such a success that word got out Fanny was responsible and soon many famous people were knocking at her door. They included Dr Johnson who had already written his famous dictionary. A useful friend for any writer to know if they ever got stuck.

Fanny's new place in society was confirmed when Queen Charlotte decided to honour her by making her 'Second Keeper of the Robes'. I have no idea what this involves. It sounds like sewing on buttons and keeping things straight on hangers and certainly can't have been as arduous as being 'First Keeper of the Robes'. Nevertheless, poor Fanny's health did something that occasionally happened to women of the time – it 'broke down' and she was forced to go and stay in Surrey for a bit of a lie down. Here she met a group of French exiles including one General Alexandre d'Arblay who

was a delight which was good but penniless which was bad. Fanny married him anyway and cracked on with her 'scribbling business', writing novels and plays to make some money. In 1794 she suffered a 'constant bilious attack' which turned out to be a son, Alexander, who she spoilt rotten.

Fanny and the Alexanders went to France where she famously underwent a mastectomy without anaesthetic which no one should read about if they are feeling at all light headed. Sadly both chaps eventually died and Fanny lived out her retirement in an Austen-like manner in Bath. Fanny was ahead of her time berating men *"who would keep us from every office, but making puddings and pies for their own precious palates!"*. Virginia Woolf called her *"The Mother of English Fiction"* and clearly it is time that she was famous again.

Fanny published four novels and eighty plays, as well as endless journals and letters. Her novel *Cecilia, Memoirs of an Heiress* had a cracking plot involving the heroine, Cecilia Beverley, being ill treated by not one, not two but three guardians, nearly tricked out of her fortune before finally marrying the man she loves. Jane Austen loved Fanny's 'scribbling' and found the title for *Pride and Prejudice* in *Cecilia*'s last chapter. Fanny herself said she had an 'incurable itch to write' which must have been uncomfy. She sometimes wrote as many as 7,000 words a day, which is a lot with a quill when you're itching.

Fanny Mendelssohn

1805—1847

F ANNY WAS THE OLDEST OF four children. Her grandfather was called Moses and her dad was Abraham which must have brought Bible stories to life as a child. When Fanny was born Abraham wrote to a friend that his wife Leah *". . . says that the child has Bach-fugue fingers"*. This is probably not the first thing most people notice about a new and mewling child but it was weirdly prophetic. Everyone will tell you that Fanny had a younger brother called Felix. What no one seems inclined to mention are her lesser known siblings Rebecca and Paul or what happened to them.

No doubt Rebecca and Paul grew up mildly irritated by how brilliantly musical Fanny and Felix turned out to be. Certainly there was hint of bitterness for years later Rebecca wrote *"My older brother and sister stole my reputation as an artist. In any other family I would have been highly regarded as a musician and perhaps been leader of a group. Next to Felix and Fanny, I could not aspire to any recognition"*. Instead of fame Rebecca became part of a salon which I think we now know means something cultural and not a place to have your hair done.

Meanwhile Fanny and Felix were in a fugue frenzy of education. They were both taught by the composer Carl Friedrich Zelter. He was friends with the develish writer Johann Wolfgang von Goethe no doubt because they were both German and famous which gave them a lot to talk about. In 1816 Zelter wrote a letter to Goethe introducing Abraham Mendelssohn to the poet in which he singled Fanny out as the kid to keep an eye on.

"He has adorable children," he wrote, *"and his oldest daughter could give you something of Sebastian Bach. This child is really something special."*

That Bach thing kept coming up but meanwhile, when Fanny was seventeen, she fell in love with a portrait painter called Wilhelm Hensel. No one thought this was a good idea as Hensel was poor and the Mendelssohns had a bob or two. William went off to Italy to study colouring-in while Fanny stayed behind doing scales. Abraham was less than encouraging about his daughter's future. He wrote to his Bach-like daughter saying that while he thought it likely that Felix would make a career of music "*. . . for you it can and must be only an ornament*". To this infamous note of discouragement Felix added his own voice cautioning against Fanny publishing her works under her own name. He wrote: "*From my knowledge of Fanny I should say that she has neither inclination nor vocation for authorship. She is too much all that a woman ought to be for this. She regulates her house, and neither thinks of the public nor of the musical world, nor even of music at all, until her first duties are fulfilled. Publishing would only disturb her in these, and I cannot say that I approve of it.*"

In October, 1828, Wilhelm Hensel returned from Italy. He found "*. . . Fanny grown from a gay girl of seventeen to a brilliant young woman of twenty-two, surrounded by a circle of intimate and admiring friends*". Going from gay to brilliant is not a transition which many girls make in modern times and he was delighted. His paintings were doing well and they were allowed to marry and the following year Fanny and Willie produced their one and only child, Sebastian Ludwig Felix Hensel.

Ever the caring brother, Felix continued protecting his sister by publishing a number of Fanny's songs under his own name. His worldwide fame took him to Buckingham Palace where Queen Victoria wanted to share her delight in her favourite of his songs and he had to confess it had been written by his brilliant sister.

In her lifetime Fanny composed 466 pieces of music and gave one public performance. She died of a stroke aged forty-one, a few hours after rehearsing Felix's cantata *Die erste Walpurgisnacht* for a private performance. Six months later Felix passed away too.

Tattooed Ladies

Lydia, oh Lydia, say, have you met Lydia?
Lydia the tattooed lady
When her muscles start relaxin'
Up the hill comes Andrew Jackson
Lydia, oh Lydia, that encyclopaedia Lydia, the queen of tattoo
For two bits she will do a mazurka in jazz
With a view of Niagara that nobody has
And on a clear day, you can see Alcatraz
You can learn a lot from Lydia

HUMAN BEINGS HAVE BEEN DECORATING themselves for centuries. When Ötzi the Iceman was dug up in 1991 in the Alpine Ötz valley in the Alps not only was he found to have been born about 3300 BC but he had about fifty-seven tattoos. How he would feel about now being one of the few men in a book of *Heroines & Harridans* is hard to say. He looks a tough old chap but that may just be because no one wears well under the Alps.

Tattoos have been around for longer than anyone thought to call them that. Egyptian mummies had them but, not many people realise, so did actual mummys. If there were a Tattoo Hall of Fame (and there virtually is) it would be full of lovely ladies from the past with names like Celly'd Astra, Artfuletta, La Bella Angora, Lady Viola, Froeken Ingeborg Sweden, La Salome and, of course . . .

Nora Hildebrandt

NORA HILDEBRANDT WAS AMERICA'S FIRST professional tattooed lady, which was not an entirely random career choice as her father, Martin Hildebrandt, was America's first professional tattoo artist and he probably got bored of an evening. Tattoos are not cheap so Martin probably found it useful to keep a calling card in the family.

Mr Hildebrandt arrived in New York City from Germany and promptly did what no one else had yet thought of as a start-up business in the New World – he opened a tattoo parlour. Nora was born about 1857. Given the sensibilities of the time she was probably born to Mrs Hildebrandt but there is more information about Nora's right thigh than there is about her mother. Civil war broke out in America (nothing to do with the Hildebrandts) and, clearly not one to take a view, Martin began tattooing soldiers and sailors from both sides. This, it turned out, wasn't a full time business so on slow days he started drawing on his daughter.

By the time she was in her twenties Nora had 365 pictures indelibly etched into her body and began to make money out of it. As if that wasn't enough entertainment for a Victorian crowd Nora embellished her decoration by telling audiences that she and her father had been held captive by the Native American (alright, she said Indian) chief, Sitting Bull, who had forced her to have a tattoo for every day of her year–long captivity. This was a very good story. Good enough to give her a fine career touring with the Barnum & Bailey Circus throughout the 1890s.

Jean Furella

NORA MADE A LIVING FROM her illustrated flesh but Jean Furella became a tattooed woman for love. Jean fell in love with a man called John Carson and John fell in love with Jean. Sadly, something came between them. It was Jean's 'long, luxuriant, dark, silky beard'. Jean was a professional bearded lady with the unusual distinction of her beard being real. John loved her but he didn't love being the least hirsute one in a couple. For fifteen years the beard caused trouble. Mr Carson said "*I loved her, all right, but I just couldn't bring myself to make love to her. I just couldn't kiss her. It always seemed to me it would be like kissing my uncle.*"

Jean spoke to her friend, Alec Linton, who was a sword swallower (this is a classic circus tale). He suggested that she ditch the beard and become a tattooed lady instead. Following the advice of men who daily dice with death is not always sensible but it worked for Jean. She shaved the beard off and covered her body in pictures. The result was a total triumph. Jean stayed in her beloved show business and married dear, but frankly fussy, John Carson.

Betty Broadbent

BETTY WAS BORN IN 1909 in Philadelphia. Because labour laws were a tad lighter in those days, by the time she was fourteen she was working as a nanny in Atlantic City, New Jersey. This can't have been all that exciting for Betty spent her spare hours wandering the boardwalk. It was the sort of place where an impressionable young girl might by chance meet a passing tattooist and Betty met one called Jack Redcloud. He showed her the beauty of all dermatological colour and Betty's new life began.

By 1927 Betty had more than 350 designs running over her limbs and body. They were a very varied selection, from the Madonna and child on her back to Charles Lindbergh on her right leg and Pancho Villa on her left. She had quite the pin-up figure and face and was soon working for Ringling Bros. Barnum & Bailey Circus. She carried on showing off her tats for the next forty years. Presumably somewhere in Atlantic City there was a bitter child who had had to bring up himself after nanny left. Betty was one of the last working tattooed ladies in the U.S., retiring in 1967.

Artoria Gibbons, (1893—1985)

ARTORIA WORKED AS A TATTOOED attraction for thirty-five years in many circus and carnival sideshows. She was born Anna Mae Burlingston on a farm in Wisconsin, a state whose nickname is the 'Badger State'. Exciting as that might have been Anna wanted to see more of the world so when she was fourteen she left home lured by the bright lights of a carnival. She had met a tattooist called Red Gibbons whom she married. After a while Red persuaded her that the tattooed life was the way forward to financial security. In those days illustrated ladies could make a lot of money.

He began his work and soon only about 20 per cent of her body was left untouched. His work was astonishing and included reproductions of paintings by Raphael and Michelangelo with da Vinci's *Last Supper* running across her back. "*My husband done every one of them,*" she would say proudly. "*They're all masterpieces. He was crazy 'bout eyetalian painters.*"

Emma de Burgh, (toured Europe 1887—1898)

EMMA ALSO HAD THE *Last Supper* tattooed across her back. Sadly she put on weight over the years to the extent that one witness claimed all "*the apostles wore broad grins.*"

Side note – Emma's was considered one of the masterpieces of the great tattooist Samuel O'Reilly. Sam was a tattoo artist from Ireland who in 1891 patented one of the first electric tattoo machines. He died in 1908 in Brooklyn, New York, when he fell off of his house while painting it. There is a lesson here about artists and the size of their canvases.

Women as Attractions

Some people will do anything to get into show business and that included . . .

Mimi Garneau, (1890–1986)

WHENEVER MIMI HAD HER PHOTOGRAPH taken she seemed to be bending forward. That is probably because she was trying to make room for the large sword she had swallowed. It's hard to know why a girl born Hazel Kirk Thomas in 1890 near Philipsburg, Pennsylvania took up such a dangerous pastime. Perhaps she had an unfortunate incident with cutlery as a child and realised she had a special gift. Whatever the origins of her career she began guzzling steel professionally in the late 1920s. Indeed Mimi is said to have been the first person to swallow a 'neon sword' (and however attractive that sounds it is recommended not to try it at home). She toured as a side attraction for a show whose main star was a preserved whale which was hauled into local train stations on a specially built truck. Playing second fiddle to a mammoth marine mammal would make any girl happy as, by comparison, she would always look thin.

After a while, however, Mimi thought she'd have a change so took the next step in a sword swallower's career and started a flea circus. Mimi was living in Florida and got a local jeweller to make little carts for the fleas to pull and other flea-size props. She got the stars of her show slightly more cheaply off a neighbour's dog. Her new act was booked into Sam Alexander's Show at Belmont Park, Montreal. It opened to terrific great acclaim but in one of the great tragedies of show business it seems her talented Florida parasites didn't like the Canadian weather and they all passed away.

A game girl, Mimi tried every dog in town with no luck. Eventually she imported a dog from Florida only to find the immigration authorities had deloused it on the way in. Knowing she was beaten she retired. The lesson is – if you don't like fleas, go to Canada.

Lillian Francis Smith, (1871–1930)

LOTS OF PEOPLE REMEMBER THE sharpshooter Annie Oakley but Lillian may have been a little overlooked which is a shame. She was a flashy dresser and, apparently, a shameless flirt, qualities which probably put a girl in her best light while she is still alive. When she was seven she rather sensibly became bored of playing with dolls and asked her father for a rifle instead. As they lived in California he thought this a perfectly reasonable request. Lillian became a cracking shot and by the time she was fifteen she joined Buffalo Bill's Wild West Show as Oakley's rival. This may have explained why they never became friends. They did, however, meet Queen Victoria together in 1887, one of the few times Her Majesty was in the presence of guns and no grouse.

Lillian never did quite as well as Annie. Eventually she left Buffalo Bill, put on some make-up and joined Mexican Joe's Wild West as 'Princess Wenona, the Indian Girl Shot'. She spent more than thirty years performing as a sharpshooter before retiring in 1920.

Historically, of course, women's talents have never seemed as interesting as their looks and others were pressed into a show business life because of their appearance. Women like . . .

Anita the Living Doll

ANITA WAS HUNGARIAN WHICH IN itself doesn't make one into a fairground attraction. She was, however, also only 26 inches tall and weighed 13 pounds and that is the sort of stature that used to sell tickets. Promoters thought she made a 'nice change' from animal attractions and she became very popular.

She was variously billed as 'Nature's Tiniest Human Adult', the 'human atom' and 'veritable Venus'. Everyone made a lot out of the fact that someone so small was very intelligent and she was advertised as being fluent in French, German and English. No one seemed all that bothered about speaking to her in Hungarian. In fact you could probably forget the whole Hungarian thing as it was never really a selling point.

She met King George V and Queen Mary who followed Queen Victoria's example of meeting people on the fringes of entertainment. Dates for Anita are tricky but she was in Sheffield in 1911 which is a benchmark of sorts. The poor woman was said to be frightened by the attention she would receive outside the circus and was often carried under the coat of her friend, a lion and elephant trainer called Arthur Feeley.

Annie Jones, (c. 1860—1902)

PARENTS WHOSE OFFSPRING ARE TROUBLED by excessive body hair from an early age sometimes seek medical advice. Instead Annie's parents sought out the great circus impresario P. T. Barnum. Annie was born in Virginia and was troubled with body hair from an early age. So much so that by the time she was nine months old Barnum was displaying her as the new 'infant Esau' and her folks were getting $150 a week. By the age of five she had a moustache and sideburns and was well on her way to becoming America's top 'bearded lady'. She had a sort of religious theme to her career because when she toured Russia as an adult she claimed to have turned down painters asking her to pose as Jesus.

Titana the Fat Girl

PHOTOGRAPHS OF TITANA MAKE HER look rather cheery and no fatter than many a girl in a chip shop queue. Such was the popularity of fat women shows that in the 1890s five could be found at Hull Fair alone, the largest travelling fair in the United Kingdom.

Others were often exhibited because of unfortunate medical conditions like: Eliza Jenkins *The Skeleton Woman*, Leonine *The Lion-Face Lady* and Alice Bounds *The Bear Lady*.

Hairy Mary from Borneo

MARY WAS A FAMOUS FAIRGROUND attraction but she doesn't really count as she rather famously turned out to be a monkey.

Hester Thrale

1741—1821

THERE IS A LESSON IN the life of Hester Thrale for any woman who wishes to be remembered for her own talents – don't make friends with famous men. It is all anyone will talk about. Hester was friends with Samuel Johnson who knew enough words to write a dictionary and who some people say was the "*most distinguished man of letters in English history*". Anyone who mentions Hester has to talk about clever clogs Sam, which frankly casts a shadow over her own brilliance.

Hester was very bright. This was clear from the beginning when she did the one smart thing every woman should include in their life – she was born into money. Hester (née Salusbury) entered this splendid world in Caernarvonshire, Wales on January 16, 1741 somewhere 'between 4 and 5pm'. The Salusbury family may have been one of the 'most illustrious Welsh land-owning dynasties of the Georgian era' but clearly not one of their clocks was in great working order. Hester's lineage was impressive. She was the eighth great-granddaughter of King Henry VII on both sides of her family line which suggests a long history of relations who didn't bother with a very wide social circle.

Hester married a rich brewer called Henry Thrale who can't have had enough to occupy him at the office as he had both the time and the energy to provide his wife with twelve children. If anyone wonders why it wasn't Hester who was the most distinguished person of letters in English history they might like to consider what a dozen children would do to anyone attempting a cogent thought.

Hester and Henry lived in a big house in south London called Streatham Park where they made the happy discovery that London Society can be bought. Soon Henry's money enabled Hester to make friends with famous literary people like James Boswell, Oliver Goldsmith and the young Fanny Burney. Samuel Johnson became such good friends that he came for a week and stayed for seventeen years.

Hester began keeping a diary which she called *Thraliana* (an 'ana' is, of course, a collection of miscellaneous information as no doubt Sam Johnson could have told you at some length). Her diary is now seen as a great place to look if you want to find out about both eighteenth-century life and the verbose Mr Johnson but there is so much more to Hester if you look. Despite her years as a baby production line she retained a glorious zest for life.

After husband Henry sipped his final pint and headed for the great snug in the sky, the newly widowed Hester fell in love with her daughter's piano teacher, Gabriel Piozzi. He was a shocking choice. Not only was he foreign (Italian) but he was, and I hope you are reading this sitting down, Roman Catholic. Everyone was appalled except Hester who couldn't stop smiling.

Samuel Johnson was furious about the wedding and the two old friends fell out. When he passed away Hester published *Anecdotes of the late Samuel Johnson* and her legacy as a Johnson appendage was set in stone. Hester published her letters and also wrote a travel book called *Observations and Reflections Made in the Course of a Journey through France, Italy and Germany*. She followed in Johnson's linguistic footsteps but she couldn't escape his shadow. When she published *The British Synonymy or an Attempt to Regulate the Choice of Words in Familiar Conversation* critics said it must have been based on work left by Johnson.

Nevertheless, Hester lived life to the full deciding, for example, to learn Hebrew at the age of sixty-five to "*divert Ennui & pass the Summer Months away*". When she was nearly eighty they say she took a great fancy to an actor very nearly fifty years her junior called William Augustus Conway and thought of marrying him. Perhaps to impress potential paramours she held an extravagant party for her eightieth birthday when she was in fact seventy-nine. Six hundred guests attended the celebrations held in the Assembly Rooms at Bath. Despite her advancing years she earned praise for the 'astonishing elasticity' of her dancing. She died in 1821 and was buried in the churchyard of Corpus Christi Church, Tremeirchion, Wales. A plaque inside the church reads "*Dr. Johnson's Mrs. Thrale. Witty, Vivacious and Charming, in an age of Genius She held ever a foremost Place*". Not foremost enough, however, to stop Dr Johnson coming first even at the end.

Sir Walter Raleigh (the scholar, not the one with the potato) in writing about 'Johnson without Boswell' said of Hester "*It is impossible to read the Anecdotes without falling under the spell of her easy irresponsible charm*".

Eleanor
of Aquitaine

1122 or 1124 (let's not quibble)—1204

ELEANOR WAS BORN IN THE Middle Ages, a time when everyone was too busy illuminating manuscripts and jousting to write down exactly when or where she came into the world. Her parents, William X, Duke of Aquitaine and Aénor de Châtellerault, were quite the leading society lights. If early twelfth-century culture had a cutting edge they were it and too busy to write down pesky birth details.

Eleanor was a cheery, pretty child brought up speaking Poitevin and Latin and it's hard to know which would have worked better for early stand-up. She had all the normal courtly education, learning a mix of reading, music and riding with a tame hawk to kill things. When she was six her brother and her mother died which was sad but to make up for it Eleanor became heir to one of the largest and richest provinces of France which was nice. A few years later Eleanor's dad decided to make a pilgrimage to St James at Santiago de Campostela. Hoping for a blessing, along the way he stopped at a café, ate some bad eels (good eels are hard to find) and got traveller's stomach. Fearing the worse William asked his men to make sure Eleanor was looked after by Louis the Fat, King of France. The poor Duke then died. It was Good Friday in Campostela Cathedral and no doubt the Duke's last thought was to wonder what he'd done to make God so cross.

Aged fifteen Eleanor now became the most eligible bride in Europe. Louis the Fat was fantastically well named and, at the time, suffering from "*a flux of the bowels*" which can't have been pleasant for his nearest and dearest. He was, however, sufficiently delighted with news of his receiving Eleanor as an unexpected gift to clap his chubby hands and promptly arrange for her to marry his son, Louis VII. Eleanor and Louis Junior met, they married and within a week King Fatty was dead and Eleanor became Queen of France.

The new King Louis loved his beautiful wife and they had a daughter. Soon, however, Louis was in all sorts of political trouble that led to war and the usual accompanying death of entirely innocent civilians. Louis felt bad about this and thinking nothing says 'sorry' like a Crusade to the Middle East decided to pack his bags. Eleanor decided she wanted to go too and gathered together her own gang including some ladies who up until then had been quite happy with the 'in-waiting' part of their job. The crusade, as crusades go, wasn't brilliant. Louis was rubbish at soldiering and lots of people got killed. As any couple who go to war together can appreciate, Louis and Eleanor started fighting over whose fault it all was. Unlike most couples Louis was able to have his wife imprisoned for not agreeing with him.

Everyone went home on separate ships with Louis's people spreading all sorts of rumours about Eleanor sleeping with her own uncle. Eventually the Pope got tired of hearing about it. He granted an annulment of the marriage due to 'consanguinity within the fourth degree' which basically means they were distant cousins. This can't have been a surprise to anyone and comes under the heading of 'lame excuses by religious leaders in history'.

Eight weeks later ever-ready Eleanor married Henry, Count of Anjou and Duke of Normandy. (He was her cousin to the third degree but no one thought

it a very good idea to mention it.) Henry became Henry II, King of England. So now Eleanor was Queen of England which she was probably up for as she had had a practice being Queen in France. Henry and Eleanor had five sons, three daughters and apparently quite a lot of arguments. This is not surprising. Eleanor liked good manners and Henry liked spending time with his jester, Roland the Farter or more politely, *Roland le Fartere*.

Henry was so fond of this medieval flatulist that he gave him a large manor in Suffolk on condition he perform *"Unum saltum et siffletum et unum bumbulum"* (one jump, one whistle, and one fart) in the royal court at Christmas.

83

In the end I suspect Eleanor couldn't stand the noise and went back to her own city of Poitiers. Here some say Eleanor and her oldest daughter Marie spent their time encouraging chivalry and 'courtly love'. It is said that a debate was held about whether or not true love can exist in marriage and that the women decided it couldn't which suggests a hint of personal bitterness.

The rest of the story is the usual medieval royal soap opera. Everybody fought with everyone else, Eleanor was arrested and taken to England where she spent sixteen years getting to know the inside of various castles. Eventually her son Richard became King of England and she was released. She went on to rule England while Richard was crusading and, ever a game girl, aged seventy-seven, she travelled across the Pyrenees to select a wife for her youngest son John, who became King after Richard. Eventually it was all too much and she did the only sensible thing possible: she became a nun before dying and being entombed in Fontevraud Abbey as a future tourist attraction.

nd now let's jump into A&E without getting hurt first.

Women whose names begin

9-10th Century

NAMES COME AND GO IN fashion but it's fair to say that those beginning with Æ have not had a fair crack of the whip for some time. History, however, is littered with women at this end of the alphabet with many more sensible than a two-vowel start to a name might suggest.

Take Æthelflæd who was so keen on the letters A and E resting together that she used them twice in one name. She was born in the ninth century and very wisely was incredibly well connected. She was the daughter of Alfred the Great, the sister of the King of Wessex and, no doubt attracted by his own penchant for vowels, married Æthelred, King of the Midlands which was then known as Mercia. Sadly the Danes decided they fancied places like Derby and Leicester and invaded. At this point Æthelred either got sick or was killed or took up stamp collecting as he rather disappears from history.

LEFT: The celebrated Æxminster Tryptich.

86

Fortunately all that hanging about with royalty had rubbed off on Æthelflæd and she immediately took charge. ◉◈ The people called her 'Myrcna hlæfdige' which can't have been easy for anyone who had been drinking and which means 'Lady of the Mercians'.

◉◈ Lots of people know about Boudica routing the Romans and forget about Æthelflæd who was a great English warrior queen leading her chaps into battle and trying to get rid of the dastardly Danes. ◉◈ Æthelflæd died in Tamworth where there is a statue of her holding a sword and clearly telling a child to amuse himself as she's got to go to war.

Then there was Ælfthryth. She lived from about 945 and I don't mean quarter to ten in the morning. ◉◈ The daughter of Ordgar, Earl of Devon, Ælfthryth was born with the perfect combination of luck — good genes and a silver spoon in her mouth which is a nice for a baby but sounds uncomfy for the mother. King Edgar heard about the lovely Ælfthryth and sent a man called Æthewald to see if she was beautiful enough to marry. Æthelwald thought she was and married her himself. Edgar did not take well to this and had Æthelwald killed.

◈ This does not sound like the perfect start to any marriage but Ælfthryth went on to become either King Edgar's second or third wife but no one can remember. ◈◉◈◈ I am guessing third because it's usually about then people lose track.

◈◉◈ Whatever her place in the marital pecking order, Ælfthryth was the first king's wife that we know of who was crowned Queen of the

Kingdom of England. She went on to become mother of King Æthelred the Unready (which must have been annoying on school mornings) and most likely arranged the murder of her stepson King Edward the Martyr. ❧ I never met King Edward but I would imagine the martyr bit might have pushed any stepmother to the edge. ❧ Æthelred pleasingly grew up to marry a woman called Ælfgifu of York.

Not much is known about Ælfgifu although the surname 'of York' is a slight clue. ❧ Frankly her life tells you everything you need to know about women in the tenth century. ❧ We know her name, we know she was important and that's about it. ❧ She was described as being 'of very noble English stock' which makes it sound like Æthelred discovered her simmering on a back burner in the castle kitchen. She is usually credited as being the mother of Æthelred's six sons and as many as five daughters so it's no wonder she didn't have time to do much in the way of history. ❧ She was the mother of Edmund Ironside, King of England.

❖ So a great warrior queen, England's first actual queen and the mother of a King yet they are forgotten, which is terrible. ❧ They may have lived an æon ago but surely they deserve an ædicule (a niche) in history?

Stella Gibbons

1902—1989

STELLA DOROTHEA GIBBONS OUGHT TO have a plaque at the offices of *The Lady* for this august publication can truly call her one of their own. If you don't know her as a writer you are in for a treat although her boss may not have thought so. Stella was a fine writer but she was made to move to 'a dark little den at the back of *The Lady* premises' for making other members of staff laugh far too much. Heaven forfend such behaviour should be permitted.

This naughty schoolgirl attitude to life led Stella to become a novelist, a poet, a short story writer and a journalist. In 1932 she wrote her first novel, *Cold Comfort Farm*. It was great which is lovely but sadly it rather over-shadowed the twenty-four other novels, three volumes of short stories, and four volumes of poetry she went on to write. Perhaps if she had known that she might have stopped writing after the first book and taken up some other hobby.

Stella was born in 1902 to the delightfully named Telford Gibbons and his wife Maude Phoebe Standish Williams. You don't get many Telfords these days and Stella may not have been thrilled with hers. Her father, the Telford in question, was a doctor whose extreme devotion to his patients allegedly led him to take laudanum and whisky, a combination which even out-of-date physicians rarely recommend.

Sadly, his self-medication meant he was never likely to be put up for either Father or Husband of the Year. It is said he once threw a knife at his wife which, even with Stella's love of things rhyming, can't have been fun for the family. He was also a womaniser who was 'unfaithful with a number of governesses' which is commendable only in that he seemed to pick a target for

his dalliances and stick to it. When Stella's mother Maude was forty-eight she had had enough and died. Telford did not take well to this and, ever the family man, declared at her funeral. "*Oh, she was a bitch! She never cooked properly! What I had to put up with!*" before dying himself later that same year.

Her ever-helpful rubbish childhood kick-started her creativity. Stella went on to become a writer first for the *Evening Standard* newspaper and then *The Lady*. Stella began publishing poetry which Virginia Woolf is said to have liked. Perhaps spurred on by this favourable critique Stella began work on a novel originally entitled *Curse God Farm*. Her *Lady* colleague, Elizabeth Coxhead, probably thought the title a tad vulgar and came up with *Cold Comfort Farm*.

The book was a hit, Stella left and Elizabeth took over her job so everyone got something out of it.

Everyone raved about *Cold Comfort Farm* and Stella won the *Prix Femina-Vie Heureuse: Anglais* and forty quid at the Institute Français in London. Sadly, fame can be a curse and a possibly jealous Virginia Woolf turned on her fuming, *"I was enraged to see they gave the £40 to Gibbons . . . Who is she? What is this book?"*

This was one of the funniest books of all time. So funny it overshadowed all of Stella's other work which, rather dishearteningly, simply 'sold solidly'. Stella married, had a baby, wrote more, became a Fellow of the Royal Society of Literature but it is *Cold Comfort Farm* that endures as a legacy. They say the book and the notion that there might be *"something nasty in the woodshed"* was based on the offices of *The Lady* which may explain why many modern contributors write from home.

Marie Antoinette

1755—1793

L<small>ET'S JUST CRACK STRAIGHT IN</small> and start with the "*Let them eat cake*" story. If people remember Marie Antoinette for anything at all it is for the accusation that when the starving women of Paris clamoured for bread she suggested they scoff gâteaux instead. This oft quoted tale had its roots in a book written in 1767 by Jean-Jacques Rousseau. In it he related the story of a 'great princess' being told the peasants had no bread and who responded "*Qu'ils mangent de la brioche*". Poor Marie was only eleven at the time and still living at home in Austria speaking German. It can't have been her which just goes to show how little we all know about history and why this book, frankly, is a public service.

Marie is one of those people who even now divides opinion. She was either sufficiently annoying to make the French people leave the dinner table and start the French revolution or she was a bucket of charm . . . sorry . . . *un seau de charme*, who has been harshly judged and literally lost her head as a result.

Marie was born in Austria so she could, presumably, have become a ski instructor but she stuck instead to the family business and stayed a royal. She was born Maria Antonia and was the youngest daughter of Francis I, Holy Roman Emperor, and Maria Theresa, Queen of Hungary and Bohemia, which must've impressed in the playground.

Maria wasn't a great student and should have paid more attention to maths because it came up later in life. Her titled folks were fantastically relaxed, even letting Maria Antonia occasionally play with children who weren't royal. Sadly her dad the Emperor was so relaxed he died and soon her mother was in charge. Maria had lots of older sisters and her mother set about marrying them off. As can happen if you live in history, a whole swathe of the family died of smallpox leaving twelve-year-old Maria Antonia as the only potential bride left in the family. It was decided she should marry her fourteen-year-old second cousin (once removed), Louis Auguste, who was Dauphin of France. Various Frenchmen came to meet Maria and immediately got someone to straighten her teeth.

The young couple were married in Vienna but Louis was a busy man so Maria's brother Ferdinand stood in as the groom at the ceremony, which is never a great start to any marriage. Maria Antonia was renamed Marie Antoinette and sent off to her new French folks. Both Louis and Marie were teenagers and it took them seven years to consummate the match. Louis's impotence was the talk of the town which can't have helped.

At first Marie, who was very pretty, was terribly popular with the people but not always a hit with other courtiers who had a general bias against Austrians. Meanwhile Louis spent his days hunting and making locks as a hobby which probably didn't help provide pillow talk. Marie did what many a rich, ignored wife has done and took to shopping and gambling.

Louis's dad died, Louis took a number and became King Louis XVI and Marie became Queen. No one knows quite how but eventually the King and Queen had a daughter. Marie kept busy and tried to encourage everyone to wear less make-up, dress more simply and take part in amateur theatre.

Marie's greatest production was a son, Louis Joseph, but some people were beginning to think she was on the frivolous side. She had a second son to help things along but by now everyone was looking to see whether the boy looked like his father.

France was in a terrible financial state but Marie was still not interested in maths. People started speaking out against the foreign queen who spent their money. In the celebrated 'Diamond Necklace Affair' she was even accused of trying to defraud the crown jewellers. It wasn't true but the mud began to stick. Soon the chatter snowballed and Marie was being blamed for everything that was wrong in France.

Things went from bad to worse politically but Marie was busy trying to help her elder boy who had TB. The winter of 1788–89 was terrible and the price of bread rose. There were riots in Paris. No one mentioned cake. Marie's seven-year-old boy died. Everyone carried on thinking about bread. The National Assembly demanded more rights from the King. He refused. More riots. Terrible false pamphlets circulated accusing Marie of disgraceful lesbian affairs in between sleeping with her remaining son. Lots of toffs left France but Marie soldiered on. Eventually the family did try to escape but the plan was a disaster.

People started losing their heads, the royals were imprisoned and eventually both Louis and Marie were beheaded by Madame Guillotine. Her last words were *"Excusez-moi, monsieur"* after she accidently stepped on the executioner's foot. She was thirty-seven. *Un seau de charme.*

Maid Lilliard

c. 1545

HERE WE GO AGAIN WITH yet more women in history who were so feisty it's best just to pretend they never existed. This recurring amnesia occurs most frequently in the category of females known as 'The Tough Cookie' because there is nothing more annoying than a bold woman who becomes a hero.

The Scots in particular seem to have been adept at producing 'women who are not to be messed with'. Possibly the scariest was Maid Lilliard. She fought in The Battle of Ancrum Moor in 1545 during the War of the Rough Wooing, which sounds like a description of so many people's teenage years. Henry VIII wanted his son Edward to marry Mary Queen of Scots. I don't know why. Edward was only eight and Mary was three so even the chances of them playing nicely together would have been slight. Anyway, not the man in history most gifted with the sensibilities of romance, Henry decided to send troops to knock the Scots into giving up their Queen to marriage. And so, in the name of love, many Scottish places were razed and pillaged.

When the English attacked at Ancrum Moor it is said that Lilliard's lover was killed and this made her more than a touch irritable. She attacked back and after some monumental fighting the Scots won the day. Go to the Scottish Border town of Lilliard Edge and near Dere Street you will find a monument to that ancient fury that tells you everything you need to know about what women can be like if provoked.

The inscription reads:

Fair maiden Lilliard
lies under this stane
little was her stature
but muckle was her fame;
upon the English loons
she laid monie thumps
and when her legs were cuttit off,
she fought upon her stumps.

Is it true? I don't know but I do know I wouldn't have wanted to challenge the maid on anything she claimed.

WHILE WE'RE ON WOMEN WITH tartan tempers we shouldn't forget about Black Agnes. (She wasn't actually black. She just had dark hair but may have tanned well.) Agnes was born in 1312 and grew up to marry Patrick, 9th Earl of Dunbar and March. They lived in Dunbar Castle in Scotland. Patrick was off fighting elsewhere when the English, led by William Montagu, 1st Earl of Salisbury, attacked Dunbar. Agnes only had a handful of servants but she refused to surrender. Salisbury started bombarding the place with catapults. Each time he finished Lady Agnes and her maids would dress in their finest frocks and go up to the battlements to give them a dust and shout down insults. For five months the poor English Earl tried to crack the castle but Lady Agnes held on until he went away.

No one says Agnes didn't exist but they don't agree on all the stories about her bravery. It is alleged (and often denied) that Salisbury managed to capture Agnes's brother John Randolph who was the 3rd Earl of Moray. The Englishman paraded John in front of the castle threatening to kill him if Agnes didn't surrender. Agnes looked down at her brother with a noose around his neck and shouted for them to go ahead as then she would inherit John's title. Salisbury let John go.

PEOPLE ARE ALSO FUNNY ABOUT what they will or won't believe about Kublai Khan's niece. Kublai was the Great Khan of the Mongol Empire in the latter part of the thirteenth century. This was quite a job covering as it did one-fifth of the world's inhabited land. Kublai needed people he could trust and, according to the great traveller and tell-all Marco Polo, that included his niece Princess Khutulun. Apparently she was his finest fighter and could do things with a bow and arrow that could literally have your eye out. Naturally Kublai wanted her to be happy so he tried to get her to marry. The Princess, however, seemed to like fighting and wasn't crazy about domestic chores so she declared she would marry according to the following simple rules – any man who could wrestle her and win could claim her as his bride. Any man who lost had to give her 100 horses. The redoubtable Princess . . . concluded her life unmarried with 10,000 horses.

A lie or just too true for comfort?

Bessie Colman

1892—1926

IT'S NEVER GOOD TO BEGIN a story at the end but be warned: Bessie Colman died because she was short. Before her diminutive death and a funeral attended by more than ten thousand people, she went from being born poor and obscure to a fearless flying life of fame. Beginning her story at the beginning is a little tricksy as Bessie tended to claim she was younger than any certificate agreed, but she was probably born on January 26, 1892 in Atlanta, Texas. Her mother, Susan, could be forgiven if she didn't remember what year it was as Bessie was her tenth child and there were three more still to come. With that many kids to produce it's doubtful Susan was ever upright long enough to look at a calendar.

Bessie was born a fine mix of African-American on her mother's side and part Choctaw and Cherokee Indian on her father, George's. After all the kids were born George decided he didn't like Texas and went back to what people used to call Indian Territory, but which these days prefers to be known as Oklahoma. All Bessie's brothers left home, leaving Susan with four daughters under the age of nine and no one to take out the rubbish. She and the girls were poor enough to make this a perfect story of the American dream, spending their days in the cotton fields and their nights straining their eyes trying to read the Bible in dim light. Bessie walked four miles every day to a one-room school in Waxahachie, a small town whose name either means 'fat wildcat' or 'cow manure', which just goes to show how imperfectly the American Indian was understood.

All the while Bessie dreamed of 'amounting to something'. She managed a single term at the Colored Agricultural and Normal University in Langston, Oklahoma but ran out of money. In 1915, when she was twenty-three, she moved to Chicago where her brother Walter, a Pullman porter, lived and got a job as a manicurist in the White Sox barbershop. Her brother John returned from the war in Europe and told her that French women were the best; that they were even allowed to fly airplanes. Bessie decided to become a pilot but no white instructor wanted to teach a black person and most certainly not a black woman. She needed to go to France to learn but as it would be a good idea to understand the lessons she needed to learn French. Bessie went to language school and in November 1920 left for France ready to *parler* her way to being a pilot.

The flying course at *École d'Aviation des Frères Caudron* at Le Crotoy in the Somme took ten months. Bessie did it in seven. She was now the world's first licensed African-American pilot. By the time she got back to America she was quite

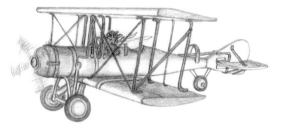

the celebrity. She began giving demonstrations of daredevil manoeuvres and getting great press. She even gave a show in Waxahachie where she insisted that there was no segregation at the main gate. She became famous giving lectures in black theatres, churches and schools but plenty of the white newspapers ignored her and it was not always easy.

Bessie could never quite afford the plane she wanted. On the evening of April 30, 1926 Bessie and her mechanic went up in her plane for a test run. Bessie was planning a parachute jump for the next day. *Warning*: here is the killer short bit – Bessie was too short to see over the edge of the cockpit so she took off her seatbelt to lean over and check where she would land. Someone had left a wrench in the plane after it had just been serviced. The stray tool slid into the gearbox and jammed. The plane failed to pull out of a dive, it spun and Bessie was thrown out to her death. She was just thirty-four.

There were funeral ceremonies held in three cities. About 10,000 people paid their last respects at the memorial service in Chicago. It would've been no surprise to her father that Texas took its time to pay due respect. Seventy-three years passed before Bessie was inducted into the Texas Aviation Hall of Fame. Former NASA astronaut, Mae Jemison, wrote "*I point to Bessie Coleman and say without hesitation that here is a woman, a being, who exemplifies and serves as a model to all humanity: the very definition of strength, dignity, courage, integrity, and beauty. It looks like a good day for flying.*"

The first woman to ascend to the skies at all was Élisabeth Thible. She was a French opera singer who is only remembered as the first woman to ascend to the clouds at all. It was June 4, 1784 in Lyon, France when Élisabeth boarded a hot-air balloon called *La Gustave*. Dressed as the Roman goddess Minerva she joined the pilot, a Monsieur Fleurant, and sang arias while feeding wood to the fire as they took off. The idea was to honour King Gustav III of Sweden's visit to Lyon. He was no doubt delighted. She turned an ankle on landing.

Monstrous Women

"Some French women, or monsters rather, in Michaelmas term 1629, attempted to act a French play at the playhouse in Blackfriars; an impudent, shameful, unwomanish, graceless, if not more than whorish attempt, to which there was great resort."
William Prynne, English lawyer, author and pompous bastard.

THE FIRST ACTOR THAT WE know about took to the stage in 534 BC (no one knows what month but shall we agree it was a Tuesday?). That first performer was a Greek fellow called Thespis. Soon men were shoving each other out of the way to get the best thespian parts. It took women a lot longer to take to the stage because presumably there was an awful lot of housework to do first.

For a long time being an actress at all in London was illegal so men played the women's parts. This was not always successful. There is a story of King Charles II (1630–85) going to see a play which suddenly stopped. His servants popped back stage to see what the problem was and found the actor who was supposed to play one of the women was still shaving. Charles was a keen theatre goer and, because he could do what he liked, in 1662 he decided, rather radically, to declare that only women should play women in the theatre.

This led to the 'unnatural vice' of women taking to the stage.

Margaret Hughes, (c. 1645—October 1, 1719)

MARGARET OR PEG HUGHES IS often credited as the first professional actress on the English stage. This only goes to show what a murky business history can be. Some say it was Hughes who first trod the boards as Desdemona on December 8, 1660 in Shakespeare's *Othello,* for Thomas Killigrew's new King's Company, while others claim it was a woman called Anne Marshall. For the purposes of expedience, we shall give the credit to Hughes as this is a short book and there isn't time to fight.

What we know for certain is that this life-changing performance took place at Killigrew's theatre in Vere Street, which he had converted from a tennis court and which probably still had a faint smell of the gym about it.

It's not clear how Peg Hughes came up with the idea of taking to the stage but she was a great hit. The only man to ever write a diary in London, Samuel Pepys (1633–1703), thought she was "*a mighty pretty woman*" which, as is the way of the world, didn't hurt her career. Not only the first actress Peg was probably also the first woman to benefit from the 'casting couch'.

Prince Rupert, Duke of Cumberland or 'Rupert of the Rhine', was an interesting fellow. Pepys (you can't mention anyone from the time without checking what Sam thought) said he was the "*fourth best tennis player*" in England. This is a curious Restoration list for anyone to be on but perhaps it was this love of tennis that first drew him to the Vere Street theatre. Soon, however, he was in love with Peg. This did her no end of good for by 1669 she had became a member of the King's Company. This gave her both status and immunity from arrest for debt which is frankly the absolute most any actor could wish for.

Rupert, busy as he was with the Rhine, never married Hughes but he gave her a daughter and lots of money. Sadly he died and Peg had a tricky time brought on, rather pleasingly, by her gambling habit.

Elizabeth Barry, (1658—November 7, 1713)

LIZ WAS ANOTHER GREAT ACTRINE of the Restoration period. Her dad was a Royalist soldier but the family were careless enough to lose their wealth so she was brought up by Sir William Davenant who was a friend of her father. Unlike Margaret Hughes, young Liz was no raving beauty and heaven knows why she wanted to act but she undertook her first part in 1675 when she played Draxilla in *Alcibiades* by Thomas Otway. She was seventeen and instantly terrible. Otway fired her. By now, however, Liz was beginning to have the one thing a struggling artist requires – connections.

John Wilmot, 2nd Earl of Rochester, was in love with her and it is said that he coached her into becoming a brilliant actress. (It is also said, of course, that Noah once built a boat by himself when he was 600 years old so we must be careful what we believe.) Whatever the cause Liz went on to have a long and brilliant career with her first big success being the part of Leonora in Aphra Behn's *Abdelazer* (July 1676). The great actor Thomas Betterton said that her acting gave "*success to plays that would disgust the most patient reader*".

No one knows the full story of these English actresses of the Restoration period but the legend is that Liz once stabbed a real-life rival in the back during a production of *The Rival Queens* and as the gossip remains delicious it is worth repeating. According to one account, Miss Barry took the part of Roxana in the play while an actress famous for her 'breeches parts', Elizabeth Boutell, played Statira. The women were in dispute about a particular veil which Boutell had been given "*by the Partiality of the Property-Man*" and during a staged fight Barry "*. . . struck with such Force, that tho' the point of the Dagger was blunted, it made way through Mrs Boutel's Stayes, and entered about a Quarter of an Inch in the Flesh.*"

Miss Barry never married and in 1709 retired from the stage.

The Rival Queens, *or the Death of Alexander the Great*
The play written in 1677 by Nathaniel Lee seems to have caused no end of trouble with some people blurring the line between fact and fiction. The blank verse tragedy concerns the jealousy of Alexander's first wife, Roxana, for his second wife, Statira.

Anne Bracegirdle, (c. 1671—September 12, 1748)

Anne played Statira in the winter of 1692. Captain Richard Hill was so taken by her performance that he became jealous of the actor William Mountfort who appeared with her. On December 9, Hill led a gang who attacked and killed Mountfort in the street which, for an actor, is even worse than a bad review. Hill fled to France which might not be every Englishman's idea of a good time.

Rebecca Marshall, (fl. 1663—1677)

Actresses loved to play Roxana and none more so than 'Beck' Marshall. Rebecca was said to be very beautiful and twice she had to ask protection from King Charles II against "*obstreperous men in her audience*". Presumably the King had better things to do (mainly with Nell Gwyn) but Beck was a woman to arouse passion. Her performance in *The Rival Queens* so aroused Aubrey de

Vere, Earl of Oxford that he attacked her sedan chair and tried to abduct her. He failed but he was nothing if not a trier so he had another go. Eventually the Earl even managed a 'false' marriage with Rebecca which can't have been fun for anyone.

Actresses through the ages

Finding actresses at all in early theatre is tricky mainly because men preferred to put dresses on themselves and play great heroines. Then the church decided all acting was a disgrace and so for hundreds of years women had to do all their play acting at home. Ironically it was the church that revived acting when a theatrical vicar decided to stage a 'Miracle Play'. Still it was only boys. Even with Shakespeare it was only boys on the stage. Juliet was a boy. Ophelia was a boy. Even Cleopatra was a boy. No wonder they all died.

Foreign Women

The first professional contract for an actress that we know about belonged to Lucrezia of Siena in October, 1564. Lots of those early women didn't improve mainly because the parts written for them by men were so dull. The first celebrated actress was the 'divine Vincenza Armani' who started mucking about on stage in 1565. Sadly she was poisoned by a former lover which suggests drama in every nook and cranny of her life. It was Charles I's Queen, Henrietta Maria, who brought a French acting troupe to London which included women performing in Britain for the very first time. Everyone was pleasingly horrified.

$\Delta^7 u_x = 0.$
$U_z = a + bx + cx^2 + dx^3 + ex^4 + fx^5 + gx^6,$
$F(x, y, z, \log x, \sin y, x^p, \&c.),$
$F(x, y, z, \&c.)$
$\Delta^n u_z = 0.$

Augusta Lovelace

1815—1852

ADA LOVELACE WAS MANY THINGS but the one thing she wasn't supposed to be was a Daddy's Girl. Ada's mother, Anne Isabelle Milbanke (known to her friends as Annabella), made the mistake of falling in love with a moody poet. A poet who probably set the benchmark for moody verse-making. Annabella was smart, but not smart enough to resist the charms of 'mad, bad and dangerous to know' Lord Byron. They married, Annabella got pregnant, Ada was born and a month later the great Romantic poet left England to improve his reputation by eventually dying somewhere foreign.

Annabella kept her daughter away from her dishy father and took no chances of allowing the paternal genes to come to the fore. She brought Ada up very strictly, learning maths and music and presumably always avoiding words that rhymed. Ada wasn't all sense and science, however, for in her youth she contracted an illness that required her to spend three years lying down. Whilst recumbent she designed fanciful boats and steam flying machines and spent more time looking at industrial diagrams than might be thought healthy. She also dreamt of meeting Mary Somerville, the author of a celebrated book on mathematical astronomy called *The Mechanism of the Heavens*.

You may have guessed that her dream came true or she might not really have been worth writing about. When Ada was seventeen she made friends with mathematical Mary and the two of them sat about being thrilled by numbers and sums. All life is about connections and Mary knew Charles Babbage who was Lucasian Professor of Mathematics at Cambridge which is apparently quite high up in the maths game. One evening at dinner he was explaining his new calculating machine which he called the 'Difference Engine'. No one knew he was about to become the 'father of the computer' as it was a paternity position that had yet to be considered. Ada loved the sound of the engine and soon she and Babbage were writing frenzied letters to each other.

Ada did the other things she was supposed to do – she married a man called William King who inherited a title. They became the Earl and Countess of Lovelace and had three kids but Ada's mind was still on yet another of Babbage's calculating machines, this time called an 'Analytical Engine'. It was much more complicated than the first one and hardly anyone knew what he was going on about. It was essentially the first computer but there was no Google to explain it so Ada wrote explanatory notes called *"Sketch of the Analytical Engine, with Notes from the Translator"*. In her treatise she showed that she not only understood the engine as well as its inventor but had a much clearer idea of what it might be used for in the future.

She suggested writing a plan for how the engine might calculate 'Bernoulli numbers'. (These were a sequence of rational numbers which were discovered in 1712. No one knows where they had been hiding before then.) This plan is now regarded as the first 'computer program' and makes Ada the world's first computer programmer, a thought which makes some geeks hot under their nylon collars. Babbage loved her, saying she was *"that Enchantress who has thrown her magical spell around the most abstract of Sciences and has grasped it with a force which few masculine intellects could have exerted over it"*. Enchantress or not her notes were printed under the initials AAL thus hiding her gender.

Despite her mother's best efforts Ada clearly had a big streak of her father. There were several scandals of love and she was alleged to have been quite the drinker. Indeed she is said to have considered writing a scientific study of the effects of opium and wine rather pleasingly gained from her own experiences. She also liked the horses and died with £2,000 in gambling debts, which is more than a million pounds today. Poor Annabella. Ada eventually fell out with her mother over Annabella keeping her from Byron. The links between Ada and the father she never knew are curious. He died, aged thirty-six, possibly of therapeutic bleeding used to try and cure illness. Ada died aged thirty-seven, possibly from therapeutic bleeding to try and cure illness. She was buried beside him.

Ada passed away long before any of the great calculating engines were built but the notes by this 'Enchantress of Numbers' were said to have inspired the legendary and tragic computer scientist Alan Turing's work on the first modern computers in the 1940s. In 1979 a software language developed by the U.S. Department of Defense was named 'Ada' in her honour – not bad for a girl born in 1815.

You can't mention women and computers without recalling Rear Admiral Grace Murray Hopper (1906-92). She was an American computer scientist and Navy officer. She was the person who enabled computers to understand English rather than just maths. She also discovered the first 'computer bug' – a moth which got trapped in her giant machine.

Lady Mary Wortley Montagu

1689—1762

LADY MARY ONCE SAID *"Life is too short for a long story"* so let's crack on to the end. Her dying words are supposed to have been *"It has all been most interesting"* which is as good an introduction to a life as one might ever find. She was born Mary Pierrepoint, the daughter of Evelyn, Earl of Kingston back in the days when no one thought Evelyn a sissy name for a boy. Mary went on to become a celebrated writer, an advocate for women's rights and the person who introduced smallpox inoculation to England, all of which does indeed sound most interesting.

Her father had one of the largest private libraries in England, no doubt helped by owning a large part of the country to keep it in. By 1710 Mary was ready for marriage and two men turned up as possibilities – Edward Wortley Montagu and Clotworthy Skeffington. Clotworthy was clearly heading for the pages of a P. G. Wodehouse novel so Mary didn't want to marry him. She wasn't mad keen on Wortley either but they eloped anyway and set about doing the necessary actions to produce a son called Edward.

Wortley became an MP and Lady Mary became the toast of London. She was witty and she was gay but not in an Alice B. Toklas sort of way. She became friends with the glitterati including the Prince of Wales and the poets

Alexander Pope and John (also) Gay. For a laugh the verse makers and Mary wrote 'court eclogues' which were satirical poems which not everyone found funny. Lady M's brother died of smallpox and she contracted it herself. The disease left her scarred with pitted skin and suddenly she was less the toast of the town and more the sort of leftover bread you use to make pudding.

Just in the nick of time her husband got a job in Constantinople and off they went to have a daughter and a lot of Turkish food. Lady M learnt Turkish, made friends and learnt about the practice of inoculation against smallpox which was called '*variolation*'. (It was probably called something else in Turkish which no doubt could be fun to look up for yourself.) Variolation involved taking live smallpox virus from a smallpox blister from someone with a mild case of the disease and giving it someone who hadn't even thought of it yet. Lady M had her son inoculated and soon was telling everyone about it. People in London were not keen partly because Mary was a woman and so what would she know and because the procedure was, well, Turkish. Eventually she got Caroline, Princess of Wales to help promote the idea. This worked a treat as there is nothing like a patronising royal to get things done. Without Mary's keenness on the subject Edward Jenner's later pioneering smallpox vaccine might never have been accepted. It still took, however, more than thirty years before Mary was congratulated for bringing the practice to Britain.

While she was ligging about the Ottoman Empire, a famous Empire made up entirely of upholstered footstools, Mary wrote a lot of letters home which eventually led to endless women deciding travelling and telling others about it would make a fine career. Alexander Pope wrote to her a lot until they had some falling out. No one knows what it was about although some said he professed love to her and she responded by roaring with laughter. Historically this has never been a popular reply with any man and it led Al to write lots of horrid poems about her. They say the pen is mightier than the sword but no doubt occasionally he wished he could have just slapped her.

Meanwhile Mary had other things on her mind. Her favourite sister, the Countess of Mar, turned out to be a shilling or two short in the mental health department and Mary spent some time trying to rescue the Countess from her husband Lord Grange, who was less than sympathetic. In 1739 Mary decided she needed a gap year. She left her husband, went abroad and never saw him again. As marriages are on the whole better conducted in the same country, eventually they got divorced. Scandal continued to dog her and she worried that a hint of her sister's madness might have rubbed off. Her daughter ran off with someone she didn't approve of and her son caused endless trouble. Having led a most unusual life eventually Lady Mary did something utterly conventional and died.

She sounds a jolly sort who was always busy, seeing everyone and everything and not caring what anyone thought of her. When she was sixty-nine she confessed she had not looked into a mirror for eleven years. Her biographer, Louis Kronenberger, who called her 'the most interesting Englishwoman of her century' said "*There is the unforgettable story of her being told at the opera that her hands were dirty, and of her answering: "You should see my feet."*"
Most interesting.

Great quote from Lady M –
"*No entertainment is so cheap as reading, nor any pleasure so lasting.*"

Sacagawea

c. 1788—1812

ANYONE WHO STUDIES AMERICAN HISTORY will know about *The Lewis and Clark Expedition*. As the name suggests it involved an expedition led by two men called Lewis and Clark. My goodness they were brave, travelling thousands of miles from North Dakota to the Pacific Ocean as they explored the western United States. What the name fails to point out is that the person who helped the men to survive was a woman called Sacagawea. Perhaps the expedition should have been called *The Sacagawea Expedition in which Lewis and Clark tagged along*.

No one in the eighteenth century thought the life of a Native American was going to be interesting enough to make a note of the details so Sacagawea's early life is sketchy to say the least. We do know that she was born into a tribe of the Lemhi-Shoshone people in what today is the state of Idaho. Idaho's modern nickname is 'The Potato State' but Sacagawea's tribe was called *Agaidika* which means 'Eaters of Salmon' and suggests their diet was far superior in the early days.

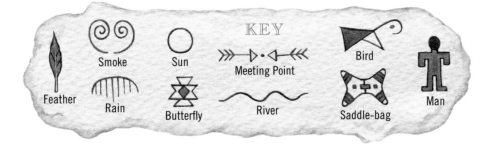

When she was about twelve Sacagawea was kidnapped by some naughty other tribe and several people were killed. A year later a Canadian trapper with the delightful name Toussaint Charbonneau, decided she was old enough to marry. Charbonneau must've been quite energetic because he not only married Sacagawea but also another young Shoshone named 'Otter Woman' who presumably was equally versatile in the water and on land. Soon Sacagawea was 'with child'.

Meanwhile the two Captains Meriwether Lewis and William Clark, had been commissioned by President Thomas Jefferson to go and find out what there was west of Washington. On their own the men got as far as North Dakota (where Sacagawea was now living) and built a small and rather draughty fort. They hired Charbonneau as an interpreter but then realised how useful his wife Sacagawea might be as she spoke Shoshone and there were Shoshone ahead. Clark liked her skills but couldn't get the hang of Sacagawea's name so he called her 'Janey'.

Sacagawea gave birth to her son Jean Baptiste Charbonneau and a few weeks later everyone headed off up the Missouri River. The men can't have been brilliant at canoeing because one day all of L & C's journals and records fell out the boat and 'Janey' had to rescue them. She spent the rest of her time bartering for the horses the men needed and finding Native Americans who had been over the Rocky Mountains before. It was a tough trip. There was so little food they had to eat candles. Perhaps because the whole thing was getting on his wick Clark failed to cover himself in suitable gentlemanly glory. Sacagawea had been saving a piece of bread for her son but it had got wet and gone a little sour. She gave it to Clark and he ate it with great satisfaction and no thought for anyone else's hunger. Sacagawea carried on finding roots for them all to eat and making clothes for all the men. She even gave up her own beaded belt so the explorers could use it to trade and bring home a present for the President.

Clark's journal entry for November 20, 1805 reads: "*one of the Indians had on a roab made of 2 Sea Otter Skins the fur of them were more butifull than any fur I had ever Seen both Capt. Lewis & my Self endeavored to purchase the roab with different articles at length we precured it for a belt of blue beeds which the Squar—wife of our interpreter Shabono wore around her waste . . .*"

Poor Clark – terrible manners and worse spelling.

On the way back Sacagawea said she knew the area and advised Clark to cross into the Yellowstone River basin at what is now known as Bozeman Pass, a route later selected as the best place for the Northern Pacific Railway to cross the continental divide.

The expedition covered thousands of miles. It was very tough on the men. Sacagawea? She was only fifteen when they set off and managed the whole thing with a brand new baby on her back. Once she was home Sacagawea had a daughter and in her mid-twenties is thought to have died of 'putrid fever' which doesn't sound nice at all. She never received a penny for her work on the Expedition. Her son was brought up by Clark.

Slightly randomly, it would seem, in 2001 then President Bill Clinton gave Sacagawea the title of Honorary Sergeant, Regular Army.

Mary
Edmonia Lewis

c. 1844—1907

EDMONIA WAS BOTH MARVELLOUS AND marvellously irritating. Marvellous because she managed to be both the first African American and the first Native American woman to achieve fame and recognition as a sculptor in the international fine arts world and irritating because there is so much we don't know about her.

Edmonia had a complicated background and she liked nothing better than to fiddle with her own back story. It's fairly certain that her father was Haitian of African descent, while her mother was of both *Mississauga Ojibwe* (that's Native American) and African descent. This gave Edmonia a marvellous melting pot of possible influences which she embellished in later life. She told people "*My mother was a wild Indian, and was born in Albany, of copper colour, and with straight, black hair. There she made and sold moccasins. My father, who was a negro, and a gentleman's servant, saw her and married her. I was born at Greenhigh, in Ohio. Mother often left her home, and wandered with her people, whose habits she could not forget, and thus we her children were brought up in the same wild manner. Until I was twelve years old I led this wandering life, fishing and swimming and making moccasins.*"

In fact Edmonia was probably born in New York and her parents both passed away in fairly quick succession when she was nine. She and her older brother,

Samuel, went to live with her mother's sisters who sold Native American craft to tourists visiting Niagara Falls.

Edmonia needed help in order to study and Samuel provided this by growing up to be a successful businessman and gold prospector. In those days no one was very keen on educating either women or non-whites so Edmonia went to Oberlin College, outside Cleveland, Ohio, which was one of the few places not to be quite so sniffy. That didn't mean, however, everyone in town was cheery about African-American-Native people.

It was winter in 1862 and snow had fallen. Edmonia was sharing a place with two classmates, Maria Miles and Christina Ennes, and all three thought they'd like to go sledging. Edmonia made some spiced wine and sadly both Mary and Christina became very ill. The doctor was called and he diagnosed that the women had been poisoned with cantharis. This is a kind of dried beetle that was used either to remove warts or as an aphrodisiac which is the kind of dual purpose drug everyone could do with in their bathroom cabinet. Maria and Christina survived but it was a close run thing. Edmonia was beaten up by some unknown assailants and then arrested for poisoning her friends. She was defended by John Mercer Langston, the only practising African-American lawyer in the Oberlin area. When she was acquitted she was carried from the courtroom on the shoulders of her friends, mostly white.

Ohio having proved less than fun, Edmonia moved to Boston to study with a well-known sculptor, Edward Augustus Brackett. Starting small Edmonia carved a woman's hand and sold it for $8. A year later she had her first solo exhibit. She was inspired by the lives of Abolitionists and Civil War heroes and was soon creating portraits of lots of social reformers with a bit of Hiawatha and Minnehaha on the side. Soon Boston was not enough and

Edmonia headed for Italy. She sailed to Rome in 1865 with her passport bearing the words "*M. Edmonia Lewis is a Black girl sent by subscription to Italy having displayed great talents as a sculptor*".

She loved Rome and soon had many artist friends and her own studio along, presumably, with a wide selection of hammers and chisels. She began to make a lot of money and tourists started dropping in to see what she was whacking out of marble. In 1876 she created a massive sculpture called *The Death of Cleopatra* for the major 1876 Centennial Exposition in Philadelphia. The piece was made of 3,015 pounds of marble and showed Cleopatra slumped in a chair clearly not feeling too clever. Thousands of people went to see it.

It was a sensation.

All seemed well but art is a fickle beast and eventually Edmonia's neoclassical style went out of favour. No one really knows what happened to her, although she is thought to have died in Hammersmith Borough Infirmary in London. She never married.

The story of *The Death of Cleopatra* is curious. It was a large item for someone to lose but for 120 years it went missing. Edmonia couldn't sell the giant work so it was bought by a race-horse owner for the grave of a horse called Cleopatra at Harlem Race Track in Chicago. Eventually the racetrack became a golf course, then a World War Two torpedo plant, and finally, in the early 1970s, a U.S. Postal Service facility. Edmonia's statue was dragged away to a contractor's storage yard where a local fire inspector caught sight of it. He got his son's Boy Scout troop to clean and paint it. Next Marilyn Richardson was working on a biography of Edmonia and heard there might be one of her works in Chicago. She tracked Cleo down in a storeroom in a local shopping mall sitting amongst paint cans and old Christmas decorations. The statue is now restored to its former glory and in the Smithsonian American Art Museum.

Blessed Hildegard of Bingen

1098—1179

THE WORD 'BLESSED' IN FRONT of anyone's name usually means they were on the saintly side unless, of course, it's followed by the word 'Nuisance'. When Hildegard was born in 1098 no one seems to have noted down the date, while absolutely everyone knows she died on September 17, 1179. I don't want to start by suggesting that Hildegard was a Blessed Nuisance, it's just odd when no one remembers your birthday but everyone can recall when you popped your clogs.

Hildegard was also known as Sibyl of the Rhine which makes her sound like a landlady in a slighty Fawlty Germanic boarding house. In fact she was a top nun, founding monasteries at Rupertsberg and Eibingen. Her CV lists her as a *"writer, composer, philosopher, Christian mystic, German Benedictine abbess, visionary, and polymath"* which was probably both impressive and a bit annoying on convent quiz nights. Apparently in her spare time she supervised 'brilliant miniature illuminations'. No one really does this fine work any more but it involves lighting up very small buildings to music.

Hildegard was raised in a family of 'free nobles'. (Which used to be given away in medieval cereal packets.) Her parents, Hildebert and Mechthilde, already had nine kids by the time Hildegard came along so when she began

having 'visions' they tried to give her away. In the end they found a nun (who obviously didn't have any children) called Jutta who was willing to take her and raise the child in a place with high walls and heavy prayer commitments. Jutta also had visions so the two got along famously, seeing things no one else thought were there.

Everyone decided it would be nice for Jutta, Hildegard and their invisible friends to be walled up together in a small room with just one tiny window. Just to show everyone what fun this was, a priest held a rather cheery funeral service while the bricklayers shut them in. Soon Hildegard was learning how to play church music and having a great time while Jutta dealt with take-aways being sent in and less than holy waste being sent out. Hildegard must have been aware that it isn't easy for two women living together in box room for she began doing apothecary work devising a marvellous recipe for relieving wind.

The sad part – Jutta died. The good part – Hildegard came out of her tiny starter home and took over the nunnery. Clearly a little twitchy to travel, she asked the boss bishop if she could move the nuns to Rupertsberg. He said no and Hildegard immediately went to bed claiming God had paralysed her because he was so unhappy with the decision. Why it was like a miracle because soon the girls were all off to Rupertsberg where the place became visions a-go-go. Hilde alternated between being too poorly to help around the place and busy writing down words sent from God.

Hildegard began writing and, in fact, was the first person in the world to think of *The Morality Play*. This is like any other play except the audience is supposed to feel bad at the end. One of her more impressive scribblings was called *Ordo Virtutum* or *Play of the Virtues* which was packed with improving lessons and probably not all that many laughs. The play

has parts for 'the Anima (human soul) and sixteen Virtues'. There is also, rather pleasingly, a speaking part for the Devil. Given that there were twenty nuns in the convent this must have left two of them without parts to do the stage management. Hilde was no fool.

The tunes she composed are what is known as 'monophonic'. Even saying the word 'monophonic' suggests something not entirely toe-tapping. It means a composition with just one melodic line. A bit like a medieval version of Justin Beiber. She also wrote a cycle of songs called the *Symphonia armoniae celestium revelationum*. Again we're in that monophonic area but apparently the tunes were soaring and considered cracking at the time. About seventy of her tunes are left behind which is about as many as any medieval composer ever managed before dying of something preventable.

Being a polymath she also wrote at least seventy poems and nine books. There are also a hundred letters but there may have been more as any correspondence with tradespeople has been sadly lost. Perhaps her most interesting oeuvre (apart from the books of visions which, frankly, go on a bit) were her volumes on the natural world. Both *Physica* and *Causae et Curae* look at nature, including big stuff like the cosmos and smaller stuff like stones. She was the Anita Roddick of her day.

By the time she was middle-aged everyone must have thought she was too clever by half at which point Hildegard invented an alternative alphabet. Anything alternative seems to have been a little out of her normal sphere as she was quick to condemn what she called "*the misuse of carnal pleasures*". Despite a strong streak of the prude there is no question that Hilde was a corker for her time. She preached when women hardly spoke, she wrote when no one else had thought of it and she was New Age before they had even finished with the Old one. Blessed.

and finally . . .

On the
Subject of Soup

Having reached the end of our historical smörgåsbord of women we, The Two Sandies, are now both a little anxious that something more sustaining might be required. Man cannot live by bread alone which is why women invented soup in the first place. Archaeologists are able to declare that the first person to make soup did so about eight thousand years ago. They cannot tell you it was made by a woman but it almost certainly was. The fledgling broth maker would first have had to weave a watertight basket of some kind, then gather large rocks and heat them in order to boil water and finally gather enough plants to create a meal. We know with certainty that this kind of multi-tasking was only done by female gatherers. The men were far too busy discussing the bison who got away and looking at spear catalogues.

Soup is good for you. Indeed the word 'restaurant' comes from the French for 'food that restores' and originally referred to a soup sold in the street which was said to make consumers feel much perkier. Soon perky people were opening whole shops to sell soup and it wasn't long before they added main courses and puddings to the menu. One of the first cookbooks, and certainly the first published in the U.S. was *The Compleat Housewife, or, Accomplish'd Gentlewoman's Companion*. It was written in 1727 by Eliza Smith and she was keen to get everyone making bisques and broths.

Often the most successful soup is made with ingredients the chef happens to have to hand. We have tried to make such a meal for you but are very aware just how much has been left out of the pot. Perhaps in addition you might have liked something sweet such as a chocolate chip cookie (invented by Ruth Wakefield, bless her) or a drop of something pleasing like a beer, a drink which from the beginning of time was brewed by women. (The word 'bridal' comes from 'bride ale', the beer brewed by women for their weddings.)

Sadly we've run out of time. As we close our small restaurant of heroines and harridans it is possible that we have exhausted the food analogy but please know – we have merely skimmed the surface of great women who deserve to be remembered.

There is so much left still to be devoured.

Barbara Palmer

Elizab...

omoe Gozen ALICE B. TOKLAS

Annie Jones

Dame Eth...

Pope Joan

Artoria Gibbons

Marie Stopes

Matilda of

Ta...

Eleanor of Flanders

quitaine

Æ...

Lady Eastnor

Heroines & Harridan...

Lillian Francis Smith

Mary Edn...

Hester Thrale

Emily

ILLIAN FRANCIS SMITH

Hua Mulan

Rebecca Marshall

Lady M...

Elizabeth Barry

Que...

Elizabeth I

Titana the ...

Woodville...

da Lovelace ANITA THE LIVING DO...